IDEAS
Triumphant

Books by Lawrence Lader

Margaret Sanger and the Fight for Birth Control (1955)

The Bold Brahmins: New England's War Against Slavery (1961)

Abortion (1966)

Margaret Sanger: Pioneer of Birth Control (with Milton Meltzer) (1969)

Breeding Ourselves to Death (1971)

Foolproof Birth Control: Male and Female Sterilization (1972)

Abortion II: Making the Revolution (1973)

Power on the Left: American Radical Movements Since 1946 (1979)

Politics, Power, and the Church (1987)

RU 486: The Pill That Could End the Abortion Wars and Why American Women Don't Have It (1991)

A Private Matter: RU486 and the Abortion Crisis (1995)

IDEAS
Triumphant

STRATEGIES FOR SOCIAL CHANGE AND PROGRESS

LAWRENCE LADER

SEVEN LOCKS PRESS

Santa Ana, California

Seven Locks Press
P.O. Box 25689
Santa Ana, CA 92799
(800) 354-5348

Individual Sales. This book is available through most bookstores or can be ordered directly from Seven Locks Press at the address above.

Quantity Sales. Special discounts are available on quantity purchases by corporations, associations, and others. For details, contact the "Special Sales Department" at the publisher's address above.

Printed in the United States of America

Library of Congress Cataloging-in-Publication Data
is available from the publisher
ISBN 1-931643-17-2 (hard cover)
ISBN 1-931643-15-6 (paperback)

Cover and Interior Design by Sparrow Advertising & Design

To my wife Joan Summers Lader and our daughter Wendy Summers Lader whose contributions to this book have been immeasurable.

CONTENTS

ACKNOWLEDGMENTS

I can never stress enough my gratitude to my wife Joan Summers Lader for her research, copyediting, and devoted concern that keeps me in working trim. Our daughter Wendy Summers Lader has given me her love and legal skill, particularly in tracking down case citations.

I owe much to my agent Regina Ryan for her steadfast support and to James Riordan and Bud Sperry at Seven Locks Press for their commitment to the project. Beth Diefendorf, master of research at the headquarters of the New York Public Library, has been a constant aide in solving difficult problems.

Our pro bono lawyers for Abortion Rights Mobilization, Marshall Beil, Ed Costikyan, and Maria Vullo, have given their time and brilliance unstintingly. At the University of Rochester Medical School, Dr. Eric Schaff and Dr. Steve Eisinger have run the RU 486 research projects magnificently.

The list of associates in the women's movement is long, but I particularly want to thank for their help Eleanor Smeal and Jennifer Jackman of the Feminist Majority, Gloria Feldt of Planned Parenthood Federation, Kelli Conlin of New York NARAL, Polly Rothstein of the Westchester (N.Y.) Coalition for Legal Abortion, and Susan Ricci, Barbara Seaman, and Edith Tiger of ARM.

Introduction

What makes an idea powerful? What makes it revolutionize the way we think and act and change us forever? Not many ideas have this power, but a few that do (excluding medical and scientific advances) will be examined in this book to find out where their power comes from and how they affect society, lead to an organized movement, and eventually through a law or court decisions become part of our lives. This is a historic process that is fairly new. It comes out of the American and French Revolutions and represents a sharp break from the past when all our choices were ruled by God, nature, or at least by monarchs. It is only in the last two hundred years that human beings have achieved enough control to shape their own individual destinies.

A few resounding words open this new era of ideas: "All men are created equal" proclaimed the Declaration of Independence (rewritten today as "men and women"). No words like this had ever inflamed a nation. Nothing had ever separated us so decisively from the past. This concept may not yet be won, but we had created a new society where the deepest human needs, rarely mentioned before, had suddenly emerged into public debate.

Ideas that covered the whole span from the beginning of life to the end of life would now be part of personal choice. Women were often the prime movers. Perhaps women's needs had been more suppressed. Ideas unleashed their deepest passions. Women worked furiously to escape from the bonds that once held them, and still do to a greater extent than men. Thus women are at the forefront when it comes to decisions about family size, and they often assume a leadership role about the most provocative new ideas.

Certain laws govern the emergence of ideas. Not only must the idea be imbedded deep in the needs of human beings, but the forces of history must have gathered so strongly behind it that momentum builds up. Timing is essential. With luck, an idea can take root fairly quickly. More likely, the process may take a hundred years or more. A few people or a group may be responsible for the original initiative, but they are only the agents of history. They are acting and speaking for forces that have long been gathering. They are the directors of change, steering an idea into channels that will reach the most people and establishing the machinery that will speed up its acceptance.

The ideas that affect our personal lives most acutely have almost always come from individuals or groups. Once released from the past, we have grasped hungrily at the chance to be master of our choices. Governments, to be sure, have produced such crucial ideas as Social Security, Medicare, and Medicaid. But they have been dangerously slow in grappling with ideas that change most aspects of our lives. And they usually have to be pushed into turning progressive ideas into law.

It has long been overlooked how a simple legal idea became a bedrock of capitalism. Initially, monarchs financed empire building: Prince Henry the Navigator of Portugal funded the ships that explored the African coast in 1457; Queen Elizabeth of England backed Sir Francis Drake's explorations. But the search for new wealth became too expensive even for monarchs. How could new investment be encouraged? The solution was a simple idea: Money had to be pooled from many sources. Thus, when the East India Company was founded in 1600, it built a capital of 68,000 pounds from two hundred investors. But more was needed: the protection of each investor. Again, the solution came from a legal twist soon called the corporation. An investor risked nothing but his share of stock; he could not be held liable for a lawsuit or damages. With this idea of an independent legal body called a stock corporation, the foundations of capitalism were created.

The speed with which an idea moves toward acceptance often depends on the conservative forces arrayed against it. The starting point of women's struggle for the vote could be considered the Seneca Falls Conference of 1848. It was not till 1920 that the vote was secured by constitutional amendment.

Yet, the franchise was only a small part of the explosive idea of women's equality. Equality had a multitude of facets. Women needed cohesion and organization. Betty Friedan's book, *The Feminine Mystique*, published in 1963, expressed these longings. The founding of the National Organization for Women (NOW) a few years later became the instrument for change. None of the ideas Friedan promoted were completely new, but they were forced into public debate during the turbulence of the civil rights movement and anti–Vietnam War radicalism when the country had been prepared for a strikingly new agenda.

Although Friedan's book responded to the needs of millions of women ready for a reorientation of their lives, the irony is that it ignored the most revolutionary of all ideas—the necessity of birth control. Only through controlling and planning the number of their children would women be able to seek the education they wanted and the jobs they were qualified for. Birth control in addition would add stability to the male/female partnership and help to equalize the responsibilities of family life.

Another important law governing the progress of an idea is that the essential technology for its success must be available to the public. In the case of birth control, the birth control pill and the morning-after pill eventually supplemented the first crude forms of diaphragms. The right to a safe abortion never became a mass movement until the procedure was simplified and made safer by the vacuum method and antibiotics.

No idea has shaken the country so wrenchingly as the right to die on our own terms, which only became a national debate as medical technology prolonged the lives of patients far beyond reasonable limits. In a broadening series of court cases, patients and their families have gained the right to remove life-sustaining machines from the brain dead and similar tragic cases. The next question was whether cognizant individuals who have a physical condition that renders their lives meaningless should have the right to decide when they die. These demands have built a movement. Oregon became the first base. Its extensive organizing campaign succeeded in passing legislation in 1997 (backed by the courts) that allows assisted suicide with medical cooperation following the approval of two physicians.

The historic forces guiding the progress of an idea often depend on one cataclysmic event. The basic steps leading to birth control originated in France in the eighteenth century and then were transplanted to Britain. Ironically, although the Declaration of Independence in 1776 unleashed revolutionary ideas, counterforces held back the acceptance of birth control. I will examine why so many historic ingredients made France ripe for change and why Britain was primed to deal with new ideas more effectively than the United States. Then I will concentrate on how two people in Britain—Annie Besant and Charles Bradlaugh—created the cataclysmic event that revolutionized British birth control almost overnight.

Ideas have to pass through an evolutionary process. Strategy is an essential part of this process, but the staying power of organizations behind an idea must be passed on from generation to generation. Otherwise, critical ideas may surface and disappear. It is an immutable law that no idea becomes part of the fabric of society unless enough people are permanently dedicated to keeping it functioning and powerful. Summing up Sir Isaiah Berlin's philosophy, Arthur M. Schlesinger, Jr. concluded: "Ideas are the great educators. They are the entries into mysteries of human existence."[1]

Chapter 1

BIRTH CONTROL: AN OLD IDEA REVOLUTIONIZES SOCIETY

The historic forces that made France the initiator of the birth control movement were rooted in its special political and social culture. The idea of preventing an unwanted pregnancy goes back to ancient times. An Egyptian papyrus that dates from around 1850 B.C. recommends hardened crocodile dung as a pessary and the douching of the vagina with a honeylike liquid. Another papyrus at the same time suggests placing acacia tips mixed with honey in the uterus. Soranus of Ephesus a century later cites a variety of potions to dislodge the fetus. But despite the frequency of such quixotic early prescriptions, the need to sustain fragile populations against the ravages of war, plague, and disastrous medical care blocked any organized attempts by women to make the idea of birth control a national policy. Then the peculiar circumstances of French society in the eighteenth century created a framework for drastic change.[1]

As prices rose sharply in the 1750s, the fear of poverty caused modest wage earners to limit their families. An increasing number of French were moving to the cities where the difficulty of preserving living standards required fewer children. Many bourgeois, obsessed with social status, were buying their way into the nobility and knew that too large a family would drain their resources.[2]

It was the French Revolution, however, that drove the country toward a birth control policy. Until then, the basis of feudalism had been "primogeniture and entail," which decreed that all property must be left to the eldest son or occasionally a wife or daughter. With its philosophy of rationalism and human rights, the Constituent Assembly of 1793 dismembered this ancient doctrine, and the Code Napoleon of 1804 completely eliminated primogeniture (the eldest son provision). The thrifty French refused to have their land and property divided among a dozen children and quickly reduced their offspring to two or three. The birthrate per thousand persons, which had been 38.6 in 1771, dropped to 30 by 1829.[3]

The momentum of an idea toward acceptance almost always depends on improved technology. A movement could not develop until people had the means to make family limitation work. Both Gabriello Fallopio, an Italian anatomist of the early sixteenth century, and Daniel Turner, an English expert on syphilis in 1717, promoted a linen sheath–type of condom as a protection against disease. But it was not till Casanova (1725–1798), who obsessively recorded his sexual conquests, that the romantic assets of a "little coat of very fine transparent skin" were promoted. The most persistent advocate of the condom, however, was James Boswell (1740–1795), the renowned biographer of Samuel Johnson, who constantly recorded in his diary that he had made himself "safely sheathed" with an animal membrane tied at the top with a pink satin ribbon. Condoms soon became widely advertised, one manufacturer boasting that the military could buy those adorned with their regimental colors.[4] The condom never became truly efficient until Charles Goodyear was granted a U.S. patent for vulcanized rubber in 1844. A British outlet expressed its patriotism by decorating its condoms with a picture of Queen Victoria.

The idea of birth control reached a turning point when women decided they would take charge of their own protection. Why should they trust a man to have a condom ready? The securest approach was to develop their own form of birth control, the vaginal sponge. There is no certain date of its early use in France, but Jeremy Bentham, the

English philosopher and economist, following his French travels, mentioned the sponge in a 1797 essay. Francis Place, a London breeches-maker turned politician, described it more fully in an 1822 book lauding the advantages of birth control: "An inch of sponge about an inch square being placed in the vagina—withdrawn by means of a double twisted thread or bobbin attached to it." In the same book, Place defined a second method, a tampon of "lint, fine wool cotton, flax or wheat."[5]

Although Place and a few pioneers worked hard to transplant the French birth control concept to their own country, Britain would still depend on abortion to eliminate unwanted pregnancies. Early abortion had long been accepted under civil authority, which replaced the church. Writing in the thirteenth century in his book *The Laws and Customs of England*, Henry de Bracton concluded that common law did not apply to the first twelve weeks of pregnancy. Punishment for aborting a fetus could only be administered after "animation," the point when the fetus moved in the womb (a pretty vague dividing line). Sir William Blackstone (1723–1780), author of the influential *Commentaries*, decreed that "Life begins in contemplation of law as soon as the infant is able to stir in the mother's womb."[6]

England's centuries-old tolerance of early abortion came to a puzzling halt in 1803 when Lord Chief Justice Edward Law and first Baron Ellenborough, rammed a restrictive bill through Parliament. In a hodgepodge collection of poisoning offenses, Ellenborough's statute ended the common law right of abortion before animation. Still, its wording was confused. It made a capital offense of a woman using a drug or "preparation," but it ignored surgery or other "contrivances to cause abortion."[7]

The rationale behind this bill may never be known. There is no mention of a parliamentary debate in the *London Times* or Hansard's parliamentary record. We can only assume that Ellenborough was trying to boost the British population, whose military strength had been drained by the American Revolution and Napoleonic Wars, forcing dependency on Hessian troops and other mercenaries. The meteoric rise of industrialization also demanded a mounting supply of factory and mine workers and had harnessed children as young as nine or ten. Cholera, typhoid, tuberculosis, and other diseases were devastating population growth, particularly in urban tenements. As late as 1840, almost half the children born in Manchester died before they reached the age of five. Infanticide also brought a grisly toll.[8]

It would take Francis Place to grasp the evolutionary process started in France and transform it to the birth control needs of British workers. Place was born poor in 1771, the son of a cruel London bailiff. With minimal schooling, he was apprenticed to a breeches-maker at thirteen. At eighteen, he was a proclaimed agnostic, speaking constantly at labor meetings and organizing strikes by carpenters and plumbers.

Astute at both business and labor organizing, he opened his own manufacturing shop for breeches and other clothing at twenty-eight and in two years had thirty-six men working for him. By 1817, he was making a profit of 3,000 pounds a year and retired at age forty-six.[9]

Place would devote the rest of his life to the working man and birth control, forming close friendships with such prominent intellectuals as Jeremy Bentham, John Stuart Mill, and Robert Owen and becoming such a skilled political manipulator that Whig leaders often counted on him to press the right parliamentary buttons. He campaigned for the Reform Bill of 1832 and for elementary schools for poor children. But he mainly concentrated on population. He was convinced that large families such as his own would destroy the working man and the health of his wife. He wanted people to marry young so "debauchery will diminish" and envisioned birth control as the means for workers "enjoying themselves rationally."

In 1822, Place published his landmark book *Illustrations and Proofs of the Principle of Population*. Although describing two techniques of contraception, he felt information was not enough. In a decisive step in the development of an idea, Place wanted to make sure that it reached English workers. With extensive contacts among union leaders and editors, he traveled constantly to promote both his book and a subsequent handbill, "To the Married of Both Sexes," whose price was low enough for anyone to afford.

John Stuart Mill, one of Place's disciples, handed out these "diabolical handbills" on London streets and was arrested and briefly jailed. Ironically, Mill had become a renowned thinker by his death in 1873, and London had planned a statue in his honor, only to have it blocked by Prime Minister William Gladstone on hearing of the arrest.

Ideas require a building process to crystallize public opinion. Richard Carlile, another Place disciple, risked the blasphemy laws by publishing Tom Paine and other suspect works and spent nine years in jail. Carlile wrote *What Is Love?* and *Every Woman's Book* in 1825 and 1826, which not only advocated birth control and the sponge, but demanded female suffrage and the general emancipation of women. In the United States, Robert Dale Owen son of Robert Owen and a member of Congress, pushed the birth control campaign in his 1830 book, *Moral Physiology.*

Place's pivotal emphasis on bringing contraception directly to English workers met severe obstacles. It was generally believed that birth control would destroy religion, morality, and the family structure. The *London Times* insisted it would "corrupt the morale of youth and of people generally" and "incite them to obscene and unnatural and immoral practices." Women would be debased; by removing the necessity of procreation from the sexual act, they would become little more than prostitutes. The *Times* predicted an end to marriage. One member of Parliament, A. M. Sullivan, contended that birth control "struck fatally at the foundation of civil society."[10]

What was needed in the second half of the nineteenth century to dilute these counterforces was a cataclysmic event that would completely change public opinion. That event would be the trial of Charles

Bradlaugh and Annie Besant. Curiously enough, the trial would revolve around their sale of an American book, *Fruits of Philosophy* by a Massachusetts advocate of birth control, Dr. Charles Knowlton.

Published in 1832, Knowlton's book confirmed Place's prescription for the vaginal sponge: "a very delicate piece of sponge, moistened with water, to be immediately afterwards withdrawn by means of a very narrow ribbon." But the book gave equal attention to douching. It recommended a syringe with a soft metal barrel and piston head to wash out the vagina with solutions of alum, vinegar, chlorides of soda or sulfate, or zinc. The book sold modestly, but it brought Knowlton a jail sentence of a few months at hard labor in Cambridge, Massachusetts, not because he had broken a birth control law (non-existent then), but because he had "offended morality." Nonetheless, Knowlton soon became a respected doctor in New Hampshire and a member of the state medical society.[11]

After *Fruits of Philosophy* was published in England, it stayed in print for over forty years despite small sales. Then in 1877, through a confused mix of police authority, it was banned by the government and, in a flamboyant flaunting of the law, republished by Charles Bradlaugh and Annie Besant. They had prepared for this moment all their lives: they had been steeped in controversy for years; they had constantly challenged the establishment; they were both masters of oratory, skilled in the manipulation of public opinion. Committed to birth control, they were the most noted radicals in Britain. No one else was better fitted to use their trial to inflame the country and convert millions to birth control.

Bradlaugh's status was already assured. In a lecture trip to Boston in 1873, the eminent abolitionist Wendell Phillips introduced him as the "Sam Adams of Britain." Referring to his insistence that the British monarchy be replaced with a republic, the *New York Herald* described him as the "future president of England." George Bernard

Shaw concluded, "He was quite simply a hero" who "reduced his most formidable rival to pygmies."[12]

Bradlaugh was born on September 26, 1833, the oldest of seven children of an impecunious legal clerk and nursemaid. At twelve he worked as an office boy at a dollar a week. When the local minister refused to answer his questions about the Gospels, he was befriended by Richard Carlile and became an atheist. Driven from home by a devout father, his new job as a baker's helper was quickly imperiled when a customer complained "I should be afraid that my bread would smell of brimstone."[13]

Already in debt, he joined the Seventh Dragoon Guards in Ireland where he became a figure of contempt when fellow troopers found a Greek lexicon (he was self-taught in Arabic and other languages) in his baggage. But he soon gained admiration not only for his riding and fencing but for his courage in pulling down a fence that a local landowner had built across a right-of-way to block communal access.

Bradlaugh would make a career as Britain's most notorious pleader for atheism, republicanism, female suffrage, Irish emancipation, and the separation of church and state. He barely scraped out a living from his speeches. Staying in two tiny rooms in a London slum, there was only space for a cot into which he fitted his bulky frame. He was hounded constantly. At Wiggan, bricks were thrown at him. At Norwich, he was mobbed. On the isle of Guernsey, the audience shouted "Kill the infidel!" Locked out of a hall in Huddersfield, which had already been paid for, he broke open the door and addressed a raucous crowd. When a gang of toughs tried to break up a Trafalgar Square meeting, he rode up on a horse and dispersed them. In 1860, Bradlaugh started *The National Reformer*, a journal that the government charged was blasphemous and seditious. Although untrained as a lawyer, he pleaded his own case and won. He was constantly in court either for himself or other radicals, rarely charging them a fee.

His expanding reputation made him president of the London Secular Society in 1858 and head of the national body a few years later.

Standing well over six feet with broad shoulders and a massive head, Bradlaugh had distinct enunciation and a slightly harsh voice used skillfully in sarcasm and denunciation. "His power over a crowd is something marvelous," observed Mrs. Moncure Conway. His gray-blue eyes had "depths of brilliant passion" that "could freeze your blood with terror," a listener commented.[14]

Yet, he also had the laugh of "some Titanic schoolboy" and was "full of merry jokes," two associates noted. He was especially courteous to women. He had become a good wrestler in the army and occasionally used his strength to throw a heckler out of a hall. He always dressed in black with a black silk hat and a flowing black tie set off against a white shirt. Women were strongly attracted to him and made up a majority of his audiences.

Speaking at the hall of Science in London on August 2, 1874, Bradlaugh immediately picked out Annie Besant from the crowd. She had written to him about her conversion to atheism and the prejudice against women at London University where she was denied a science degree despite high honors in exams. She was a beautiful woman with masses of soft brown hair, and they were soon traveling together on speaking tours. Her favorite topic was "The Political Status of Women." Still, yielding to the Victorian climate, they insisted that one of their children should always accompany them. Besant was separated from her husband and Bradlaugh from his wife, an alcoholic living with her family in the country, but the *Essex Standard* described them as "that bestial man and woman who go about earning a livelihood by corrupting the young of England."[15]

They made an explosive team. Although Besant and George Bernard Shaw almost certainly had an affair, there is no proof of any sexual link between Besant and Bradlaugh. Yet, she always considered him the most beloved man in her life.

Besant, who was three-fourths Irish, was born Annie Wood on October 1, 1847, fourteen years younger than Bradlaugh. She came from a distinguished family, her second cousin being Lord Chancellor. As a member of the poorer branch of the family, she was forced to follow the accepted female route by marrying early to the Reverend Frank Besant, a Church of England clergyman. His demands for obedience hardly fit this rebellious woman, and she escaped his home almost as soon as she had borne a daughter, Mabel, and a son, Digby. She would later claim he had struck her six times.

Frank Besant began furious legal proceedings to take the children from her. When Bradlaugh hired Besant as an editor of the *National Reformer* in 1874, she was immediately tarred with his image and branded an "infidel lecturer" and unfit mother. This characterization became the deciding factor in the court's decision to award the children to Frank.[16]

When they returned to the lecture circuit, crowds in mining villages greeted them with brass bands, and a parade of carts and lorries followed them through the streets. Bradlaugh had become "Our Charlie" to many of England's workers. Karl Marx, who considered him a "huge self-idolater," was always incensed that Bradlaugh refused to accept his socialist teachings. Yet, as they approached the brink of a decision in 1877 to go to trial over *Fruits of Philosophy* and make the population issue the fulcrum of national controversy, it was Besant's ego that dominated. Bradlaugh was uncertain whether a test case would produce climactic results. Besant pushed him on with her passion and feminist commitment. She was convinced the case would make her the first renowned feminist in British history.[17]

AN IDEA REACHES AN EXPLOSIVE POINT: THE BIRTH CONTROL TRIAL OF BRADLAUGH AND BESANT

Charles Bradlaugh and Annie Besant determinedly sought arrest in 1877 for publishing *Fruits of Philosophy*. They knew they could go to jail and threaten "almost the existence of my future life," as Besant wrote. Yet, they were addicted risk takers, and the possibility of promoting the first real birth control campaign stirred their sense of history.[1]

We can never know whether a gathering momentum of forces makes its own hero at the opportune time, or whether a potential hero awaits the perfect opportunity to turn an idea into an epochal event. Certainly the birth control movement would have progressed without Bradlaugh and Besant, but they speeded up the process by twenty or thirty years.

The secular societies had been selling about one thousand copies a year of *Fruits of Philosophy* for over forty years with no complaints from the British government. James Watson had been the publisher from 1833 until his retirement. Then Charles Watts took over his business.

It will never be known what quirk of official censorship was roused by the sale of the book at a Bristol store. Even at the trial, it was never revealed who brought the charges. Still, Watts was arrested on January 8, 1877, and sentenced to two years in jail. Rather than make a freedom-of-the-press case, he decided to plead guilty and was let off with a twenty-five pound fee.

Bradlaugh was furious at any infringement of the press. "I deny the right of anyone to interfere with the full and free discussion of social questions affecting the happiness of this nation," he announced. But he didn't like the book particularly and doubted it would fit his birth control strategy.[2]

Besant, always a careful researcher, decided that the book had ample medical merit. She urged it could gain more status with a new foreword by Dr. George Drysdale, an advocate of contraception in his book *Physical, Sexual and Natural Religion* and a cofounder with Bradlaugh of the Malthusian League in 1861. Besant was proud to be the first British woman to support birth control. She welcomed the chance to add to her notoriety. She insisted that *Fruits of Philosophy* be republished, and they immediately established the Free Thought Publishing Company to do the job.

With his flair for legal confrontation, Bradlaugh sent a copy of the new edition to the chief clerk of the magistrates court. He added a note that they would be selling copies for sixpence at their office on Stonecutter Street on April 7, 1877, from 4 to 5 P.M. The public, too, had been informed. A crowd gathered, and eight hundred copies were sold in a few hours. Bradlaugh and Besant were promptly arrested under the Obscene Publications Act.

They were well aware that the trial was not just about contraception, but would be the first open challenge to English standards of sexual morality. Dr. William Acton had set the tone in 1857 by proclaiming, "Decent women have no sexual feelings." Now the solicitor general at the trial would brand *Fruits of Philosophy* an "indecent, lewd, filthy, bawdy and obscene book, and the test of it is that no human being would allow that book on his table, and no decently educated English husband would allow even his wife to have it." For good measure, he added that it would "debase and degrade the relation of the sexes."[3]

The nexus of the drama was punishment for sexual pleasure. The solicitor general would claim that the object of *Fruits* is "to enable a person to have sexual intercourse, and not have that which in the order of Providence is the natural result of that sexual intercourse." The horror was even worse for the young, "the boy of seventeen and the girl of the same age—that they might gratify their passions" and not worry that "conception followed." Morality had always required that the objective of sex was procreation. The possibility of sex for pleasure would polarize Britain.[4]

Again seeking maximum exposure, Bradlaugh moved that the trial be upped from the Central Criminal Court to the Queen's Bench, where it would involve the highest judicial officials in the land. The government may have been so certain of winning that it agreed. Starting on June 18, 1877, and running four days, the trial was held before the Chief Justice Sir Alexander Cockburn, with Solicitor General Sir Hardinge Giffard as prosecutor. Every seat was taken in the "ancient, vast echoing space of Westminster Hall," as one journalist described it. Most reporters were even denied entry. A crowd of 20,000 waited outside.

Bradlaugh and Besant defended themselves, and their speeches were often hours long. They could be florid and emotional, but generally struck a detached, scientific note. They called on Dr. Drysdale and Dr. Alice Vickery for a medical analysis of how large families affected both the mother's and the children's health. When Cockburn asked whether the book would "incite sexual or libidinous" reactions, Drysdale, amid a burst of laughter, said it would have a contrary effect.[5]

Besant stressed that "if the book was obscene, then many medical works were so." And Cockburn had to agree it was a "dry, physiological treatise." Besant reached her oratorical heights when pleading for the poor, claiming they had printed *Fruits* because the "cry of the poor was in our ears, and we would not permit the discussion of the population question, in its practical aspect, to be crushed."

Dominating the courtroom with her piercing gray-blue eyes and lovely oval face, she hammered at the theme that it was not birth control but huge families that were immoral. "It is immoral," she insisted, "to bring children into this world when you cannot clothe, feed, or educate them."[6]

Bradlaugh, who had linked poverty and contraception almost fifteen years before in his pamphlet, "Poverty and Its Effects on the Political Condition of the People," claimed that without birth control, "human society is a hopeless and insoluble riddle." In a thundering conclusion, he cried, "You can never have true liberty so long as men are steeped in poverty."[7]

The most noteworthy impact of the trial, basic to Bradlaugh's strategy, was the nationwide coverage every day by almost every newspaper. The words "family limitation" and "contraception" had never been mentioned before in the press. Now they appeared on every breakfast table, and the subject was debated in editorials and letters. From March to June of 1877, 125,000 copies of *Fruits* were sold, and hawkers peddled imitation and pirated copies on the streets.

Although a few liberal papers like the *Leicester Weekly Post* urged that the subject "ought to be open for discussion," most condemned this assault on morality. "Millions [were] corrupted by this work," preached the *Liverpool Mail*. Contraception would "corrupt the morals of youth and of people generally," added the *London Times*. "Moral purity and elevation of sentiment," concluded the *Manchester Examiner and Times,* "were even more valuable than life."[8]

Although Chief Justice Cockburn praised the defendants for their honesty and courage and remarked with seeming bias "I think a more unjust accusation never was made," the jury came down with a strangely jumbled verdict. "We are unanimously of the opinion that the book in question is calculated to deprave public morals," they announced, "but at the same time we entirely exonerate the defendants from any corrupt motives in publishing it."[9]

Cockburn determined that the book, at least, was guilty and asked Bradlaugh and Besant to promise to halt all sales. They refused. Angered, he sentenced them to six months in jail with fines and recognizances coming to about 1,400 pounds. Bradlaugh and Besant claimed they later learned six of the jury had intended to exonerate the book. But Arthur Walter, son of the chief owner of the highly antagonistic *Times*, working through an ultrareligious foreman, had convinced them to switch their votes. When Bradlaugh moved for a writ of error, Cockburn held up their prison terms.

None of this discouraged people from seeking birth control information; it served mainly to heighten public awareness. Bradlaugh and Besant lectured the night of the verdict at the Hall of Science to a crowd that overflowed by the hundreds into the streets. The majority were "young females who appeared to fully endorse the opinions enunciated by the lecturer," *Reynolds Newspaper* noted. On a tour of the country, crowds followed them everywhere. In six years *Fruits* would sell 600,000 copies in Britain and the United States, proof of the important role the media plays in promoting ideas.[10]

To expand this mounting audience, Besant wrote her own book that year, *The Laws of Population*. In addition to the sponge it recommended a rubber cervical cap, and in later editions, a vaginal pessary. Contraceptive devices were now sold openly in drugstores, and leaflets often distributed from door to door. They were advertised widely in newspapers, although occasionally disguised as a cure for "all cases of irregularity." In the next few years, Besant's book would sell 175,000 copies.

In 1878, a three-judge court of appeals completely exonerated Bradlaugh and Besant. Admittedly, their decision was on the technical point that the solicitor general had not clearly and expressly spelled out the grounds for prosecution. *Fruits* itself could no longer be banned since the court expressed "no opinion whether this is a filthy and obscene or an innocent book."

In the progress of any idea toward acceptance, the established authorities often lag far behind the momentum of history. There is a repeated rhythm of force and counterforce , and one of the foremost counterforces was the medical profession. *Lancet,* a medical journal, argued in 1887 that "If this evil [birth control] is to continue, at all events it shall never exist as a sidewing of the healing art." Many physicians considered birth control a danger to a woman's health. As late at 1921, Dr. Mary Scharlieb, honored by the government with the title of Dame for her service on the venereal disease commission, made the astonishing announcement that "Nations with no restraint on sex are liable to become effeminate and degenerate."[11]

Still, forces soon combined to ensure birth control. The Compulsory Education Act of 1878 severely restricted the employment of child labor and diluted the economic rewards that a family would gain from working children. Compulsory attendance at school was raised to age twelve in 1899 and, in some districts, to age fourteen in 1900. Any employment of minors under age eleven would soon be banned, and from age eleven to fourteen, they could only work half time or on alternate days. Consequently, in Lancashire child employment fell 40 percent by the turn of the century and 33 percent in Yorkshire.

Another strong motivation toward birth control was the rising emancipation of women. They were taking factory jobs not just as a step to independence, but to supply the means for better clothes, home furnishings, and entertainment. With the prosperity of the 1870s increased opportunities meant that in textile towns, such as Blackburn, women would hold almost half the jobs. Fifty-nine percent of women aged twenty to twenty-four years were soon employed.

Parents from the middle class were demanding higher education for their children, particularly to qualify for coveted civil service posts. Smaller families obviously lowered the costs. Even the underprivileged grasped the advantages of birth control, and Besant proudly noted the flood of letters she had received from " the wives of county clergymen and curates—thanking and blessing me for showing how to escape from the veritable hell in which they lived."[12]

The decisive factor was the Bradlaugh-Besant trial, which Dr. Ethel Elderton concluded "had revolutionized the sexual habits of the English people." Her landmark study, made by University of London team just after the turn of the century and published in 1914, conclusively showed that the impact of the trial had sharply cut the birthrate after 1877. From 1871 to 1875, the average birth rate was 35.5 children per 1000 women. By 1914, it had plummeted to 14.4 per thousand.[13]

The pattern was consistent in every area. Bradford dropped from 26.2 per thousand in 1851 to 13.8 in 1901; Bury from 23.9 to 13.8; Lancaster from 24.3 to 16.2 The only exception was Liverpool with its high quota of Irish and Catholic dockworkers.

Elderton continually found through in-depth interviewing that women had not just been influenced by the trial but by Bradlaugh's subsequent lectures in the area. Although birth control had largely been embraced by the middle and upper classes, she reported that "Even among the poor, knowledge of preventive means is pretty well spread." In Scotland, she found the decline has been nearly as great as in England." She concluded it was now "exceptional to find more than one or two children to a family."

The medical profession finally had to accept the sweeping effects of this social revolution. In his presidential address to the British Gynecological Society in 1904, Dr. John W. Taylor announced: "Instead of families of six to twelve to eighteen children, we see more often the so-called family of three or four or one."

Bradlaugh would be plunged into one more tempestuous conflict. In 1880, Bradlaugh had been elected to Parliament from Northampton. Although a few categories, such as Quakers, Jews, and Moravians, had previously been excepted from the standard oath, atheists must have been considered too far beyond the pale for consideration. When Bradlaugh refused to swear "on my true faith as a Christian," he was barred from his seat.

Six years of absurdity and farce ensued. Northampton reelected him in April 1881. But Parliament vacated his seat again, and ordered ten policemen and four messengers to drag him down the marble stairs. His injured arm remained bandaged for weeks. It was the first time an elected member had been kept out by brute force. After protest meetings across the country, he was released from his prison in the Clock Tower.

Bradlaugh was reelected for the third time in 1883 and tried a new ploy. He administered the oath to himself, but was refused his seat. Reelected again in 1884, Bradlaugh had the advantage of a new speaker who cut off all debate. On January 13, 1886, Bradlaugh inscribed his name on the roll, shook the speakers hand, and was seated without incident.

Meanwhile, the historic forces that the Bradlaugh-Besant trial had crystallized were augmented by two events. Dr. Wilhelm Mensinga in Germany developed a rubber, occlusive pessary with a spring-loaded rim that would remain a model for contraception for many decades. Dr. Aletta Jacobs opened the world's first birth control clinic in Holland in 1879.

Bradlaugh made a distinguished record in the House as a spokesman for labor, education, and the emancipation of India. When he was dying in January 1891, the House honored him by expunging from the record all resolutions that had previously excluded him. Indian nationalists made up one of the largest groups of mourners at his funeral, including a slim law student named Mohandas Gandhi. Convinced she had cemented her status as Britain's most flamboyant campaigner for birth control and women's rights, Besant moved to India. She would become a determined advocate of the philosophic-religious cult of theosophy for the rest of her long life.

Chapter 3

THE AMERICAN ENIGMA: WHAT HISTORICAL FORCES PRODUCED MARGARET SANGER

The trial of Besant and Bradlaugh that helped cut the British birthrate in half between 1877 and 1914 had no parallel in the United States. When Margaret Sanger burst upon the scene in 1914, she brought a revolutionary vision of feminist emancipation. Victoria Clafin Woodhull had touched upon free love but was tainted by her journalistic muckraking and lawsuits in the previous century. Sanger immediately grasped the need for a massive revolt. In the first issue of her newspaper, *The Woman Rebel,* she demanded that women could only achieve "life, liberty and the pursuit of happiness" when she made herself "absolute mistress of her own body." Sanger not only insisted that women organize against "enforced motherhood," but her fiery language was applicable to the abortion rights campaign of 1966 and still provokes tumult in the twenty-first century.

Sanger was a unique and volcanic figure. She had a radiant beauty that would attract such lovers as H. G. Wells and Havelock Ellis. Her eyes were wide-set, gray, and almost dreamy. Her hair, reflecting her Irish ancestry, was a flaming rust. Her voice had a soft silvery tone, and she had the habit of tilting her head to one side when she talked so that the listener was convinced he was getting her total attention. If her ideas were radical, she purposefully took on a conservative aura in public appearance by dressing in black with a white lace collar around her throat. The *New York Tribune* at the time described her as a "demure, rather shy-looking young woman."

This was an image she nurtured since her real objective was to blast away America's calcified attitudes on sex, birth control, and the role of women. Her dominant side was tough and brash. She had a mystic belief in her own righteousness. She had a furious energy that would never give up until she had crushed all obstacles in her way.

The complex issue is why the gathering forces behind birth control centered on Sanger. Why did she become the dominant figure in the incipient movement when others like Mary Ware Dennett and Emma Goldman were also propagandizing for birth control? Dennett, who came from a wealthy Boston family, hardly competed with Sanger because of her modest approach of changing the anticontraception laws at the ballot box rather than rashly breaking them. Goldman, however, who spoke out before Sanger, was a serious contender.

A plump, dark-haired rabble-rouser of Russian-Jewish background, Goldman was an impassioned speaker and the darling of a vigorous part of the labor movement, the Industrial Workers of the World (the Wobblies). She was an anarchist who campaigned for economic justice dosed with Marxism, workers' rights and women's issues. Significantly, in her journal *Mother Earth*, she had been pushing contraception since 1906, years before Sanger. There is a picture of her with Dr. Ben Reitman, her tour manager, lover, and also an anarchist, in front of a family limitation billboard in Butte, Montana, on June 24, 1912.

In his authoritative study of birth control published in 1936, Norman Himes, a Colgate University professor, totally ignored Goldman. Reitman wrote him, complaining, "Margaret imitated her [Goldman] and denied her. Emma was the first person in America to lecture on birth control." Both statements are correct, but Himes never made the correction. Sanger and Goldman stayed friendly allies for a while until Sanger decided that Goldman's bruising image made her a detriment to the movement. During the Communist scare of World War I, Goldman was deported by the government to Europe, which removed her from an increasingly bitter feud.[1]

The forces that would plunge Sanger into birth control were quickly discernible after her birth in 1879. Her mother, confined by constant pregnancies, bore eleven living children, and was so weakened that she died at fifty. Although Sanger adored her father, Michael Higgins, she resented that this large family had destroyed her mother's health. Her father was an antireligious, Anglo-Irish freethinker. Her mother was a devout Roman Catholic. The tensions between them confused and destabilized Sanger's youth.[1]

Sanger's radical learnings were inherited from her father. He was a disciple of Colonel Robert Ingersoll and an audacious freethinker and opponent of the Catholic Church. When her father invited Ingersoll to speak at their hometown of Corning, New York, and the local Catholic church denied them the hall already paid for, Sanger's antipathy to the church became deeply rooted. Her father was a stonecutter whose frequent, gravestone commissions from the church were now halted.

From her childhood, Sanger always connected the poverty of the workers at Corning with their ever expanding families, who occupied decrepit houses in town while the rich lived in mansions at the top of the hill. Later, her stomach would always convulse when she passed through Corning on a train. Yet, ironically, it was the Corning glass company and the Houghton family that would supply one of Sanger's firmest allies in birth control, Katharine Houghton Hepburn, mother of the actress.

Sanger's daring and independence marked her youth. She became a heroine among her peers by frequently tiptoeing across a railroad bridge when one slip would have plunged her to her death. She insisted on escaping the limitation of local education and got herself admitted to the private Claverack school, wheedling the necessary funds from older, working sisters.

But it was the Lawrence, Massachusetts, strike of 1912, essentially run by the Wobblies, that showed her she had the power to instigate a mass movement. The textile workers of Lawrence received miserable wages, lived in crowded hovels, and were laid off constantly. Their food dwindled during the long drawn-out strike, and the Wobblies decided that their suffering children had to be moved to friends in New York City. Sanger, who had a nursing degree, was put in charge of the project. She collected clothes for hundreds of children, organized their train trip, had them met at Grand Central station by a delegation of unions, and marched them triumphantly to a rally at Union Square. Sanger's achievements in the children's project were an integral contribution to the winning of the strike.

Sanger started as an organizer for Local No. 5 of the Socialist Party of New York. In 1913, she worked with the Wobblies organizing the Paterson, New Jersey, textile strike, which cemented her friendship with John Reed. Buying his Cape Cod cottage later, she claimed that the money he got enabled him to cover the Soviet revolution and to write the landmark *Ten Days That Shook the World*.

Sanger would soon shift from radical politics to advocating birth control. She was not the first to promote birth control and was certainly influenced by early advocates. Although the medical profession insisted that contraception must be a doctor's decision (the American Medical Association did not approve it until 1937), many doctors supported it before Sanger. The *Michigan Medical News* and the *Cincinnati Medical News* carried detailed articles in 1882 and 1890. Dr. Sydney Elliot of Boston demanded in a book that childbearing must be a deliberate, not a chance haphazard conception. In New York, Dr. William J. Robinson urged that birth control be taught to medical students. Dr. S. Adolphus Knopf linked contraception to maternal health. In his presidential address to the AMA in 1912, the esteemed Dr. Abraham Jacobi, father of pediatrics, branded the laws against birth control "grievously wrong and unjust."

Still earlier advocates included Robert Dale Owen (1801–1877), the son of Robert Owen who was the most enlightened of British factory owners. He emigrated to Indiana, founded the utopian colony of New Harmony, represented his state in the U.S. Congress, and published *Moral Physiology*, the first American book preaching contraception. Owen influenced Knowlton's *Fruits of Philosophy* a year later, which became the storm center of the Besant-Bradlaugh trial.

Dr. Frederick Hollick (1818–1900) lectured nationwide on contraception. Dr. Edward Bliss Foote (1829–1901) introduced the "womb veil" of India rubber, predecessor of the vaginal diaphragm. Moses Harman (1830-1910) was jailed for describing contraception in his magazine, *Lucifer, The Light Bearer*. Colonel Ingersoll (1833–1899) insisted in his lectures that science "must put it in the power of woman to decide for herself whether she will or will not become a mother."

But these early advocates were mainly male doctors who had neither the time nor the ability to rouse a mass feminist movement. Sanger realized that she, as an impassioned woman skilled in organizing, was better suited to lead. But the living conditions that Sanger witnessed as a nurse working in New York City's Lower East Side would become the dominant factor propelling her into the birth control movement. There, among the most crowded tenements in the country, she was besieged by the desperate appeals of immigrant women, overwhelmed by a constant succession of pregnancies, for some hint of how to get birth control. She was particularly appalled by the lines of poor women on Saturday night with five dollars in their hands, seeking abortions from ignorant hacks who often left them dead or maimed.

Amid this chorus of unwanted pregnancies, Sanger would undergo what she called a mystical revelation. She attributed the moment to a woman she called Sadie Sachs, seriously ill and laden with child after child, whose doctor had flippantly told her to "tell Jake to sleep on the roof." Sanger was convinced that these women had pushed her toward her mission. She claimed she neither ate nor slept while the critical decision of her life boiled inside her. She had been called to be a feminist savior. Her whole being must now be concentrated on building a mass movement of women. Everything peripheral would be wiped out in the process of making herself the voice of feminine emancipation.

Sanger's personal revelation, of course, must be balanced against the historical forces that were ready for a Herculean figure to pull all the pioneering strands together. The proper timing is always a key element in the success of a rebellion. Unlike Britain, where a population to meet the needs of the Industrial Revolution had been achieved by 1860 or so, the huge territory of the United States demanded an endless supply of workers for factories and farms. Although improved public health had lowered the death rate, the flood of immigrants from Europe would not fill the gap until the early 1900s. A Pennsylvania law of 1850, which made abortion a crime because "it interferes and violates the mysteries of nature by which the human race is propagated and continued," reflected the prevalent attitude toward birth control. A similar law in Wisconsin blamed it for preventing "perpetuation of the race."[2]

These historical forces had shifted drastically by 1914. The burgeoning middle class was demanding a higher standard of living, particularly education and college for their children, which could be provided for two or three but hardly ten. The middle class was also gaining access to condoms and diaphragms from friendly druggists and even longtime family doctors. In fact, the new elitist lament was that the middle class birthrate was falling compared to what Francis A. Walker called the tide of "beaten men from beaten races" immigrating from Europe. As director of the census in 1870, Walker wanted a hundred dollar tax on every immigrant. In 1902, President Charles W. Eliot of Harvard complained that the birthrate of his graduates fell 28 percent short of replacing themselves. President Theodore Roosevelt hammered at the catastrophe of what he called "race suicide."[3]

Sanger at this early point had little interest in the middle class. She was totally consumed by the disastrous impact of excessive childbearing on the poor. She had been molded by radical politics. Significantly, her first discussion of the link between poverty and family limitation appeared in a Socialist newspaper. The slogan of her paper, *The Woman Rebel*, was "No Gods, No Masters," a blistering warning to the established order.

Instinctively, she first used the strategy of confrontation to develop the birth control movement. Yet, she had neither the skill nor the foresight at the start to expand this confrontation to the level of a Bradlaugh-Besant trial. She avoided a trial by boarding a ship to England under an assumed name, leaving her husband and three children. She ordered her associates to release another pamphlet, "Family Limitation," which described specific birth control techniques and would certainly incite another indictment by the government.

Whether she ever weighed her escape against trial and jail (Knowlton was only sentenced to a few months in Massachusetts), she would never discuss the alternatives in our interviews much later. Her main concern was, "How could I leave these adorable children? It sickens me even forty years later to think of the struggle within me."

She was convinced her priority was to study the Netherlands clinics and meet Dr. George Drysdale, who had testified at the Besant-Bradlaugh trial. Still the guiding genius of Malthusianism and British birth control, he instigated an epochal moment in London by introducing her to Havelock Ellis, author of *Psychology of Sex* and other groundbreaking works. She was swept away by "his great shock of white hair, his massive head and wide, expressive mouth—all blended into one overwhelming impression that here was a veritable god."

Although she had been married since her nursing days to William Sanger, an architect and father of her children, she was consumed by Ellis. He advised her what to read at the British Museum library and met her for lunch three times a week. They soon became lovers. She

apparently had another affair with Lorenzo Portet, the literary executor of Francisco Ferrer, a Spanish anarchist who had been executed by
the monarchists in Barcelona. Sanger was putting into practice a
theme that would dominate her teachings: that birth control would
not only protect the physical health of women, but would liberate
them emotionally and enable them to enjoy the fulfillment of sex.
Mabel Dodge Luhan, whose Fifth Avenue salon Sanger had attended
in New York, wrote of Sanger that she "was the first person I ever
knew who was openly an ardent propagandist for the joys of the
flesh." Sanger had thus added a critical factor in the historical progression of the movement that would strongly influence the feminist
revolt of the 1960s.[4]

Sanger's desertion of her children to flee to London resulted in a
traumatic event that would shake her forever. In her last days in
London, she claimed that the date, November 6, kept occurring in her
dreams. She told an associate, "Something is going to happen to me
on that day that will affect my whole future." Always believing in her
mystical instincts, she booked passage to New York to find that her
youngest child, Peggy, was seriously ill with pneumonia.

It is questionable whether Sanger could have alleviated the illness if
she had not gone to England. Without antibiotics, pneumonia took a
heavy toll then. Sanger and her sister, Ethel, also a trained nurse, stayed
constantly at the child's hospital bedside. In rare moments of consciousness, Peggy would ask, "Are you back? Are you really back?" She died
on November 6, the exact date revealed in Sanger's dream.

While I was preparing my biography of Sanger, she revealed in a
handwritten memo to me the trauma of that time, which she had
never discussed before. She said she saw Peggy's spirit leave her body
and float in a dazzling white cloud over the bed. For years she could
not glimpse a child on the street or in a subway without starting to
weep. On every anniversary of Peggy's death, she would closet herself
in her room, admitting no visitors nor talking on the phone. But guilt?

It was a "hackneyed word," Sanger would write. She preferred "regret," which inferred no wrongdoing. "As to leaving the children, I knew it was a necessary sacrifice to leave them to prepare my defense."

While she was in Europe, Sanger's indictment had stirred the first debate over contraception in the press, but nothing like the storm her trial would have unleashed. Ironically, the focus had suddenly shifted to her husband, William Sanger, who had handed a copy of "Family Limitation" to one of Anthony Comstock's decoys and had been arrested. Comstock , an obsessive dictator of public morality, had pushed through a New York state law against contraception and abortion in 1869. Then in the waning moments of the 1873 Congress, without floor debate, he had sneaked through a federal obscenity statute that virtually gave him control of the mails and American homes.

At his trial in September 1915, William Sanger was offered the choice of a $150 fine or thirty days in jail after the judge branded the pamphlet "not only contrary to the laws of the state but contrary to the laws of God." When William insisted he "would rather be in jail with my self-respect and manhood," Sanger undoubtedly feared that her husband would intrude on her leadership of the incipient move- ment. Her relations with him were already tenuous. To make her escape to London even less significant, the government now decided that bringing her to trial would elevate her to martyrdom and dis- missed the case on February 18, 1916. Comstock had already avoided this nullification of his law by dying, like Peggy, of pneumonia a few months before.

Her political training at last convinced her that the next critical stage in a movement was what Marxists called the building of a "mass base." In the spring of 1916, Sanger set out on a nationwide tour. In St. Louis, newspapers reported, "1,200 Almost in Riot Over Mrs. Sanger." Although the Victoria Theater had been paid for in advance, the protests of the Catholic hierarchy made the management cancel the meeting, "giving St. Louis the worse kind of advertising," the *Post-Dispatch* commented. Sanger relished such religious confrontation. In Detroit, nine hundred women signed up to form a local birth control group. In Oakland, California, the *Tribune* reported that people "came in droves. Within a few minutes the Hotel Oakland ballroom miraculously filled."

Dr. Marie Equi described Sanger on the trip as a "little bunch of hellfire." But Sanger's purpose went deeper. She believed she had become the embodiment of women's yearnings, that she, and only she, could express their hopes for emancipation. "The most important force in the remaking of the world is a free motherhood," she stated. Her status was confirmed in her memory by daily contacts: the woman begging for birth control who knocked at her hotel door with a gift of flowers; the woman who did not have the twenty-five cent fee to attend her lecture but left her wedding ring at the box office for security. This fusion with her audience gave a relentless impetus to the campaign, which now officially carried the label of birth control, a phrase coined by an associate.

Sanger was now ready to launch a cataclysmic event to propel the movement to its next stage. She would challenge the New York state law. Section 1142 ruled that no one could supply contraceptive information. Section 1145 was a disqualifier, allowing doctors to prescribe birth control for cure or prevention of disease (always interpreted to mean the use of condoms against venereal disease). Logically, she should have found a doctor to run her planned clinic, but there is no record she approached Dr. Robinson or Dr. Knopf or any previous advocate. It might have been futile. Doctors had rarely taken a public stand and risked an arrest that would threaten their careers.

Instead, the fallback position was that she and her sister, Ethel Byrne, would run the clinic. Through raw October winds in what she called "those passionate, dangerous and menacing days," they searched for a location in Brooklyn and found one at 46 Amboy Street. They painted the rooms and hung new curtains. They drew up a handbill in English, Yiddish, and Italian announcing in part: "Mothers: Can you afford to have a large family? Do you want any more children? . . . Safe, harmless information can be obtained of trained Nurses." They tucked the handbills in mailboxes and under doors throughout the neighborhood.

After notifying the Brooklyn district attorney of the clinic's location, they prepared to open on October 16, 1916, a day bright and crisp after a long rain. It would be a day that started a social revolution in America.

Chapter 4

THE TIME GAP: WHY AMERICAN BIRTH CONTROL LAGGED BEHIND GREAT BRITAIN

Wives and many husbands came from the Brooklyn tenements and from as far away as Pennsylvania and Connecticut that day in 1916 when the first birth control clinic in America opened. Newspapers reported the "helpless tale of children that were not wanted but came in never-ending numbers." One woman told the *Brooklyn Eagle*: "I have seven children. Just now I am wondering how I am going to get shoes for them." Another said: "The priest told us to have lots of children. I had fifteen. Six are living." Sanger and her sister, Ethel Byrne, showed the women contraceptive devices and how to use them, but neither sold them nor gave them away. Securing the right contraception for the poor would remain a problem for the next few years.

On the clinic's ninth day, a woman calling herself Mrs. Margaret Whitehurst sought contraceptive information and returned the next day to announce she was a policewoman and placed Sanger, Byrne, and their assistant under arrest. "You dirty thing!" Sanger shouted, according to the *New York World*. "You are not a woman." The sisters refused to ride in a police wagon and walked to the station house, spending the night in the Raymond Street jail. Released on bail, they reopened the clinic but were arrested again.

Sanger's defense would require considerable money. She needed the wealth and status of noted families like Mrs. Lewis Delafield, Mrs. J. Borden Harriman, and Mrs. George Rublee. Although the opening of the clinic was the most radical step so far in the development of the movement, Sanger managed to make an alliance with these conservative women. They formed the "Committee of 100" in her defense, which enabled her to hire Jonah J. Goldstein, a savvy lawyer, former secretary to Governor Al Smith, and a rising power in Tammany Democratic politics.

Trying to bend the medical exception of Section 1145 of the state law to rescue two nurses, Goldstein argued that only birth control could prevent high infant and maternal mortality rates in large families. Byrne was tried first, but the judges weren't interested in sociology. On January 22, 1917, they sentenced her to thirty days in the workhouse. An inflexible, political rebel, Byrne went on a hunger strike and told the *New York World*: "I shall die if need be for my sex."

Despite incessant headlines on the European war, Byrne's hunger strike made the front page of the *New York Times* on January 26, 1917: "Mrs. Byrne Weaker. Still Fasts in Cell." The *Times* ran front page stories each day on Byrne's plight. On January 28, the *Times* reported: "Mrs. Byrne Now Being Fed by Force." It was the first time a woman had been force-fed in U.S. penal history.

The Committee of 100 packed Carnegie Hall on January 29 to protest Byrne's imprisonment, and Sanger told the audience "I come not from the stake at Salem" but from Blackwell's Island "where women are tortured for obscenity." Fearing that Byrne could be near death, the committee sent Gertrude Pinchot to Albany to see Governor Charles S. Whitman. The governor agreed to pardon Byrne if she promised not to violate the law again.

Visiting Byrne in jail, Sanger concluded that "the look of death was creeping into her glazed eyes." Her decision to promise that Byrne would not break the law again permanently established Sanger's leadership of the movement. Her worries about Byrne's death were certainly sincere, but she had effectively eliminated Byrne from the headlines and, in effect, ended her participation in the movement.

There would always be tension between the sisters after that. Byrne remained a political radical and always resented Sanger's newly acquired rich friends.

The shock value of Sanger's own trial, which began on January 29, 1917 in a Brooklyn courthouse, also established her supremacy over Mary Ware Dennett's National Birth Control League, whose genteel approach was to change the laws through the electorate.

Goldstein struggled to convince the court to parole Sanger if she promised not to break the law again during an appeal. But Sanger was adamant, insisting, "I cannot promise to obey a law I do not respect." She was sentenced to thirty days in the workhouse.

At the Queens County Penitentiary in Long Island City, Sanger refused to have her birth control confrontation make her a common criminal and fought off the guards who tried to fingerprint her. Eugene Debs, the Socialist Party organizer, wrote her, "When I think of you caged like a beast, all my blood boils with bitter indignation." On her release on March 6, she refused again to have two husky men fingerprint her by force until Goldstein convinced officials to forego this ritual. Sanger's friends met her at the prison gate, singing the "Marseillaise."

The appeals process would shortly raise the impact of Sanger's clinic arrest to the level of the Besant-Bradlaugh trial in England in 1877. Although Judge Frederick Crane of the Court of Appeals of the State of New York affirmed the state's right to prohibit laymen from distributing contraceptive information, his decision on January 8, 1918, strikingly broadened a physician's options. Writing for a unanimous court, Crane decreed that Section 1145 was "broad enough to protect the physician who in good faith gives such help or advice to a married person to cure or prevent disease." The court cited *Webster's International Dictionary of the English Language* in its definition of disease: "Causing or threatening pain and sickness; illness; sickness;

disorder." Thus a physician could now offer birth control for wide spectrum of causes beyond venereal disease.

Sanger had shrewdly timed the Brooklyn clinic as a critical step in the historical progression of the movement. She had the wedge. But unlike Bradlaugh and Besant, who lectured constantly after 1877 throughout Britain to build a birth control constituency after the trial, Sanger delayed. It was not until 1923 that she opened a birth control clinic in New York as now allowed by the Crane decision. A nation-wide chain of clinics would have provided the organized network to bring birth control to millions of women. Education was not enough. The important strategy at this point would have been to offer contra-ceptive information and devices.

Of course, the Court of Appeals, New York's highest court, only ruled in New York State. Yet, it was one of the most respected courts in the country and would have certainly influenced other courts. This was proved a year later when the Chicago Medical Institute sued the city to grant it a birth control clinic license and won.

Sanger's delay becomes even more puzzling because laws in a large part of the country did not prohibit birth control. It was not illegal in California and Oregon. Doctors were specifically exempted in Colorado, Indiana, Nevada, Ohio, and Wyoming. Although twenty-four states and the District of Columbia had obscenity laws, birth control was never mentioned. North Carolina and New Mexico did not even have obscenity laws.

Here was a rich opportunity to raise the tempo of the campaign and equal the speed with which Britain cut its birth rate. Admittedly each clinic would have needed a doctor, but although Sanger had the persuasive skills, there is no record that she tried to enlist young doc-tors in this period. She founded the American Birth Control League in 1922, which never developed any national strength. She may have wanted it that way. She kept it a New York movement tightly under her control. As a result, by 1930 when the movement could have

Long Island Medical College and senior gynecologist at Brooklyn Hospital. The establishment, represented by Dickinson, considered Sanger a propagandist. As early as 1916, Dickinson wrote, "We as a profession should take hold of this matter (birth control) and not let it go to the radicals."

Dickinson organized the Committee on Maternal Health with offices at the Academy of Medicine, but no affiliation. Its aim was to promote research on contraception. He wanted more doctors on the board of Sanger's Clinical Research Bureau, but she refused any intrusion on her independence. Dickinson insisted that Sanger get a license from the State Board of Charities, but she was turned down. They bickered for years, but Dickinson was inflexibly committed to birth control and eventually so impressed by Dr. Stone's meticulous research that he joined the Research Bureau's board and was instrumental in gaining the Academy of Medicine's approval of the Bureau and birth control in general in 1931. It was not until 1937, however, that the American Medical Association gave the final imprimatur.

Meanwhile, the Clinical Research Bureau's professional standing was immeasurably advanced when a Mrs. Anna K. McNamara applied for contraception on March 23, 1929. She was carefully examined and rated medically qualified. Three weeks later, she returned with a bevy of policemen, who arrested two doctors and two nurses on duty, rampaged the offices, and took away not just contraceptives but the case histories of 150 patients.

This was a brash infraction of the doctor-patient relationship, and Dr. Dickinson rallied the Academy of Medicine to make a formal protest. The *Herald Tribune* concluded that the "privileged relation of doctor and client ceases to exist," and Heywood Broun in his widely read column tartly suggested that, "If the medical profession fails to resent the raid . . . the physicians of this city should all consult their chiropractors in an effort to learn what ails their spines." A parade of prominent doctors, including Dr. Louis I. Harris, a former health commissioner of New

York City, all testified at the trial that Mrs. McNamara's condition "was in keeping with the spirit and purpose of the law." On May 14, Magistrate Abraham Rosenbluth at Jefferson Market Court ruled that the Crane decision on Sections 1142 and 1145 had been rigorously followed, and the case was dismissed. Ironically, Mrs. McNamara returned to the clinic a few weeks later and humbly appealed for treatment of her medical problems.

Sanger converted almost every step in the movement into a personal statement. The movement, in effect, reflected her, and she believed she thereby gave it mystique and power. "I just kept going night and day," she wrote, "visualizing every act, every step, *believing*, *knowing* that I was working in accord with a universal law of evolution—a moral evolution, perhaps, but evolution just the same. This belief, faith—call it what you will—gave me a feeling of tremendous power." It blurred her judgment in dealing with many stages of the historical process, but made her particularly adept in her confrontations with her principal opponent, the Roman Catholic hierarchy.

Although her speeches were frequently blocked by local Catholic officials (censored in Boston she sat with her mouth taped while a Harvard professor read her speech), her most notorious conflict with the church occurred at Town Hall in New York City on November 13, 1921. It was a mass meeting for the final day of the First American Birth Control Conference with such distinguished speakers as Harold Cox, a former member of the British Parliament. Arriving with Cox and others for the meeting, Sanger found her taxi halted by a milling crowd. A policeman told them the meeting had been canceled. Slipping through a side door, Sanger was boosted onto the stage. Her assistant, Anne Kennedy, informed Sanger that a police officer with a priest had told her "This meeting must be closed." When Kennedy presented a contract and paid receipt for the hall, she was told by the priest, Monsignor Joseph Dineen, secretary to Archbishop Patrick J. Hayes, that "An indecent, immoral subject is to be discussed." The officer was identified as Captain Donahue of the local station house.

As Sanger shouted to the audience, "We're going to hold this meeting," Monsignor Dineen ordered Captain Donahue to arrest her and another speaker. They were led down the aisle while the audience sang "My Country 'Tis of Thee," an ironic paean to liberty. When the arrested women refused to ride in a patrol wagon, they were followed through the streets by singing, jeering protestors. Next morning Sanger appeared in court, but Captain Donahue never showed up to press charges. The judge dismissed the case.

In a front page story published on November 14, 1921, the *New York Times* pinpointed the significance of the Town Hall closing. The *Times* stated, "The police suppression of the birth control meeting at Town Hall Sunday night was brought about at the instigation of Archbishop Patrick J. Hayes of the Roman Catholic Archdiocese." A *New York Tribune* editorial admonished: "It was arbitrary and Prussian to the last degree." A *New York Post* editorial warned, "our boasted freedom of speech is a mockery." Sanger pushed her advantage by restaging the meeting successfully at the Park Theater on November 18—the hall so jammed 3,000 had to be turned away.

Beyond the First Amendment violations of speech and assembly, the Town Hall suppression raised the question of how a church official was able through the police to force his religious dogma on a city. It was open proof that power in New York had been seized by the Archdiocese on Fiftieth street, which came to be known as the "Powerhouse," as no piece of city or state legislation could be passed without being cleared through it for decades thereafter.

Sanger was skilled at exploiting blunders in religious opposition. Such prominent banking and legal allies as Herbert L. Satterlee and Paul D. Cravath, as well as the American Civil Liberties Union, had the prestige to force city hall to set up an investigation. But after dragging on for three years, no final report was ever made, and no one was punished.

Although Sanger relished her conflicts with the Catholic hierarchy and often used it to her advantage in swaying public opinion, religious opposition remained one of the principal factors in slowing down the American movement in contrast to the rapid progress in Britain. Catholics were not only a small percentage of the British population, they also refrained from using political power as a bloc. Many of the smaller, Protestant denominations accepted birth control early in the century. The dominant Anglicans gave their final endorsement in 1930 at the Lambeth Conference of Bishops of the Anglican Church.

In the United States, however, at least a quarter of the population was nominally Catholic, and the hierarchy used this strength in incessant political intervention, against birth control particularly and against abortion rights after 1966. Because of the peculiar nature of American power blocs, the highly organized influence of bishops and priests over Catholic voters made the church a threat to every politician, well aware that 200 or even 100 votes could swing an election. The church's money, despite supposed legal restraining, amplified this influence. Sanger's dislike of the church was understandable, but she sometimes carried it to an extreme such as when she threatened to leave the country if John F. Kennedy was elected in 1960. In office, Kennedy was rigid in his separation of church and state. Sanger never made good on her threat.

American birth control was further slowed by the multiplicity of its ethnic groups. Britain was a homogenous nation with a high literacy rate; almost everyone could understand the Bradlaugh and Besant lectures and read their books. The tide of American immigrants, mainly Irish, Italian, Jewish, German, Scandinavian, and Asian, was another matter. Many did not achieve literacy for another generation and were difficult for the birth control movement to reach. Further, the movement became tainted by eugenicists in the 1920s who were accused of aiming to diminish the numbers of the poor. Sanger herself flirted with eugenicists briefly until she realized her error and eliminated their support.[2]

While American birth control struggled through 1937 to gain the approval of the medical elite, the British profession had virtually accepted it as a foundation of family structure by the turn of the century. There were a few blatant holdouts. But when Lord Dawson of Penn, the Queen's personal physician, became an outspoken advocate in 1927, British doctors stood strongly behind him just as they would support the first judicial test on abortion rights long before American doctors tiptoed into the fray.

Sanger was unable to grasp how historical forces evolve to produce a movement. She didn't recognize the need to build coalitions and concentrated too much power in her own hands. This was partly a belief in her own mystical fusion with the movement, partly a question of ego. She would resign as head of the American Birth Control league in 1929 after some of the board protested her strategy, writing to a friend that she was "released from the deadening influence of petty whispering criticism." Actually, she had no gift for consensual decisions. In all her letters and papers, and in three years of my constant conversations with her, there is almost no evidence that she ever sat down with a committee to thrash out a problem.

The result was one of the most misguided campaigns in her career. In 1929, she established the National Committee for Federal Legislation for Birth Control in an effort to pass a "Doctor's Bill" that would repeal Section 211 of the Federal Penal Code, otherwise known as the Comstock Law. Perhaps the main contribution of this campaign is that it established new leadership in local offices across the country, such as Mrs. Katharine Houghton Hepburn who ran the Washington headquarters. The Comstock Law, which prohibited mailing contraceptives, was of little importance now since individuals could carry them across state lines to clinic doctors. Further, the chances of passing federal legislation were minuscule just as a federal law on abortion rights could never have been passed four or so decades later despite crucial state laws in New York, California, Alaska, and elsewhere.

But, as far as is known, Sanger did not consult any sophisticated Washington lobbyist and plunged ahead. After two grueling years of local organizing, petition gathering, lobbying, and endless rallies, the first bill was turned down in the Senate Judiciary Committee. Another bill, which had more astute sponsorship by U.S. Senator Daniel O. Hastings of Delaware, had some chance of reaching the full Senate until Senator Pat McCarran of Nevada, a devout Catholic, asked for a recall and it died in committee.

Subsequent bills in 1935 and 1936, sponsored by Representative Walter M. Pierce of Oregon and Senator Percy L. Gassaway of Oklahoma, were killed again. Gassaway, the father of fourteen children, had personal reasons for supporting the bill: "Seven of my children died, and I lost my first wife in childbirth," he said.

This drawn-out campaign exhausted the movement's personnel and money. The only possible excuse for it, besides keeping Sanger in the limelight, was that it became a nationwide educational tool that drew thousands of new advocates to the movement and built a mass base for the future.

A *Fortune* magazine poll now showed that 63 percent of the American people supported birth control. Besides, repeal of the Comstock Law had become largely extraneous though a lawsuit known as the "One Package" case, filed on November 10, 1933, which was a critical step and should have been utilized long before. The "One Package" case came about through the mailing of pessaries from Japan to Dr. Hannah Stone at the clinic in New York. After they were seized by customs under Section 305 of the Tariff Act of 1930 (an outgrowth of the Comstock Law), a federal district court ordered them returned to Stone. The government appealed. On November 30, 1936, Judge Augustus N. Hand of the Second Circuit Court of Appeals in New York issued a momentous decision. The court not only affirmed the return of the package to Stone, but ruled that the law could not "prevent that importation, sale or carriage by mail of things which might be intelligently employed by conscientious and competent physicians for the purpose of saving life or promoting the well being of their patients." The government decided not to appeal to the Supreme Court. The prescription of birth control had been broadened to that encompassing phrase of "well being." The Comstock Law was dead although it was not until 1970 that Congress removed the label of "obscenity" from laws affecting birth control.

Sanger seemed to have reached the pinnacle of achievement. On January 24, 1937, she received the award of honor from the Town Hall Club, a distinguished New York civic association. Helen Keller would call her, "a free world illuminating spirit," and H. G. Wells, "the greatest biological revolutionary the world has ever known." Smith College would give her an honorary doctorate. Yet, in the development of an idea to successful national movement, birth control was still far short of reaching its mature stage.

Sanger's Research Bureau, with its education department maintaining a structure left over from the "Doctor's Bill," and the American Birth Control League had been at constant loggerheads. There was competition to establish new clinics; there was competition for money. The staffs of both organizations were amazingly small and underfunded. John Price Jones, Inc., a New York management firm, was called to seek an amalgamation. Two men, to Sanger's distaste, were put in charge, Richard N. Pierson, M.D., as president of the board, and D. Kenneth Rose of John Price Jones, as national director. In 1942, the organization's name was changed to Planned Parenthood Federation of America, and its offices moved to a prestigious building on Madison Avenue. Sanger was given the basically honorific title of honorary chairperson since her contacts with the Rockefellers and other monied families were hard to replace.

It was a drastic shift in direction. Sanger hated the elimination of "birth control" from the title, which signaled the end of a volcanic era. She may have courted the rich for money, but she had built the movement on a radical, feminist theology and staffed it with fiery women. Not only had men, and a developing bureaucracy, taken over, but Planned Parenthood would be dominated until the 1960s by sub-urbanites who downplayed the consuming mission of the emancipation of women. Sanger's energy and limitless dedication would be missed.

All the bulwarks were crumbling beneath Sanger. Havelock Ellis, Sanger's lover and mentor, died in July 1939. Her husband, J. Noah Slee, died in his sleep in June 1943, while her sons, Stuart and Grant, were serving overseas. In 1946, H. G. Wells, another lover, died. Yet, in these late years, she would steer the birth control movement toward the final stages of its evolutionary progress. She would organize the International Planned Parenthood Federation and concentrate on stemming the surge of world population. She would find the scientists and money to produce the first significant advance in contraception: the birth control pill.

Chapter 5

SANGER'S SEARCH FOR THE HOLY GRAIL

With all her frenzied energy, combativeness, and insight into the yearnings of women, Margaret Sanger often misjudged the historical forces behind the birth control movement that took almost thirty years from 1914 to achieve success. But in her final years, her instincts and strategy were faultless.

She saw almost immediately that the evolutionary growth of an idea depended on technology. France could never have started to limit its families in the late eighteenth century with condoms alone. It had to develop an efficient vaginal sponge, soon adopted by Britain and other Western nations, which eventually evolved to become the spring-loaded diaphragm accompanied by chemical jelly.

But Sanger wanted a more advanced contraceptive. The diaphragm required careful medical fitting. It took skill and time to insert in the heat of passion. It could be positioned sloppily, and it had a small error rate. Sanger was convinced that a pill making a woman infertile was a critical necessity. The quest for a pill obsessed her over many decades. She called it, "My search for the Holy Grail."

As early as 1915, Havelock Ellis told her about a chemical compound made in Germany. Pursuing wisps of information from city to city, she found a chemist in Friedrichshafen who had developed a potential pill that not only proved too expensive but testing had been stopped by the war. In Leningrad in 1934, she found a laboratory making a compound that supposedly produced infertility for three or

four months. Again the government, sensing the advent of World War
II and the need for increased population, had halted all experiments.
Sanger was able to bring the formula back to the University of
Pennsylvania, but two years of animal tests were inconclusive.

It was not until 1951 that Dr. Abe Stone, chief of the Clinical
Research Bureau since his wife's death, gave Sanger the first substan-
tial clue. Research in steroids had been going on at the Worcester
Foundation for Experimental Biology in Massachusetts. It depended
on the discovery by Columbia University biologists that steroids can
inhibit ovulation. But steroids in their natural form were far too
expensive. Widespread use was only possible when Russell Marker, a
noted Penn State University chemist, found a way to synthesize prog-
esterone (a steroid) chemically from the roots of the Mexican yam.

After a few trips to Worcester, Sanger recognized the validity of the
research and insisted that her friend, Mrs. Stanley McCormick, join
her. They made an irresistible team—charming, demanding, and
always holding out the lure of McCormick's money.

McCormick was the widow of the son and heir of Cyrus
McCormick of the International Harvester company. Born Katherine
Dexter from a distinguished and wealthy Boston family, she was one
of the first women to receive a science degree from the Massachusetts
Institute of Technology. She had married Stanley McCormick in 1904,
but shortly afterward he became the victim of an untreatable schizo-
phrenia. McCormick had often helped Sanger by smuggling diaphragms
into the United States after her European trips. She had made her lavish
home the center of the Geneva Population Conference. Sanger was a
constant guest at her mansion in Santa Barbara, California, and
McCormick was a steady funder of Sanger's work.

A remarkable confluence of historical forces at the final stage of the
birth control campaign brought these two women together to push the
research at Worcester. McCormick, the equal of Sanger in vision and

enthusiasm, immediately donated $100,000. She would give millions more in the next few years and millions more in her will.

The pill became a reality through the brilliance of three men: Gregory Pincus, Ph.D., and M. C. Chang, Ph. D., of the Worcester Institute, and John Rock, M.D., of Harvard Medical School. Pincus, a scientist of daring imagination with bristling, black eyebrows and bushy, gray hair crowning a high forehead, had left the Harvard faculty after being denied tenure to organize the Worcester Institute and push independent research on a picayune budget. Chang, a thin, stooped figure with an enticing smile, had left China to get his doctorate at Cambridge University, England, and came to Worcester in 1945. Pincus concentrated on blueprinting the endless variations of steroid compounds under study. Chang ran the animal testing.

Rock, an eminent gynecologist who had long specialized in female infertility, was the prototype of Brahmin courtliness with silver-white hair and ruddy skin, almost always dressed in bowtie and tweeds. Sanger considered him "handsome as a god."

Still, Sanger at first thought Rock presented a serious problem. He was a devout Roman Catholic who attended church regularly and kept a crucifix above his office desk. Yet, his religious convictions had a rebellious core. In 1931, he had publicly demanded the repeal of the Massachusetts law banning birth control and constantly urged the Catholic church to change its birth control policy. He coauthored *Voluntary Parenthood*, a book that described contraception for the public, and insisted that the new pill was simply "an adjunct of nature" and conformed to Catholic theology. Pointing out that conception could not start until the meeting of sperm and egg, Rock explained that with the pill, no egg was released but was only absorbed within the ovary. "If there is no free egg and no fertile period, there is no contraception," he concluded.

After the Worcester scientists had narrowed their research to the 19-norsteroid group of compounds, Chang completed the first successful animal tests in April 1951. Sanger and McCormick badgered the Worcester team constantly, heaping them with money and praise. When Pincus gave Rock the first pills, labeled Enovid by G. D. Searle the drug manufacturer, Rock tested them with convincing results on a group of his middle-class patients who were fully informed of their pioneering role. Far more extensive tests were done in Puerto Rico and Haiti, a practice that would later invite criticism that underdeveloped countries had been exploited. But subsequent testing in Los Angeles mitigated the attacks.

"The present pill was tested more exhaustively than any other drug in history," Pincus noted. Parrying the expected religious claims that the pill would make sex too convenient for the unmarried and especially the young, Rock, who supervised all testing, insisted, "I seriously doubt the pill has had any influence on morality."

Sanger and McCormick were so elated that they described the Worcester research at the International Planned Parenthood meeting in Tokyo in 1955. But few understood its significance until Pincus published his exhaustive study in *Science* magazine a year later. Then there was a scramble by other drug companies to compete with Searle with their own versions of the pill. The Food and Drug Administration (FDA) approved the pill for public sale in 1960.

Neither Sanger, McCormick, nor any family planning organization ever made a penny, and the Worcester scientists received modest profits as consultants to Searle. The drug manufacturers, however, gained huge new sales from the pill, and the Syntex Company, which made the synthetic steroids, along with their financiers, reaped millions.

Sanger's dogged concentration on the development of the pill assured that the birth control movement would reach its final evolutionary stage. The pill has continued to be the leading contraceptive choice of women in the United States. At least 10.4 million American women use it as of 1995. A late method is the Ortho Evra patch, worn by a woman three weeks a month and easily changed, second in popularity to the Depo-Provera shot given once every three months.

The pill's convenience has strikingly advanced access to contraception. Admittedly, a woman may occasionally forget to take one or two pills in her monthly cycle, which means she must resort to other methods at that point. Critics also cited the pill's risks and side effects, but these were minimized after drug companies reduced the hormonal content.[1]

Starting with the turbulent feminist revolt of the 1960s, the pill helped to revolutionize America's sexual mores. It shifted the responsibility for protection against pregnancy to the woman, who now, if she chose, could indulge her romantic inclinations without prior planning. The birth control movement continued to develop other methods of contraception, such as the coil and Norplant (tiny rods inserted in a woman's arm that give five-year protection, a seemingly ideal product badly mishandled by the manufacturer), but the most significant development was the so-called morning-after pill. Taken in concentrated doses within a few days after unprotected intercourse, the morning-after pill effectively eliminates any potential pregnancy; the woman never knows whether she was pregnant or not. This pill, long a standard treatment in Europe and on American college campuses, was finally approved by the FDA in 1998.

The birth control pill must rank at the top of Sanger's achievements and was the decisive step that brought to fruition the idea of readily available contraception. When Sanger donated a copy of my biography of her to the Worcester Institute, she inscribed it: "To Mrs. Gregory Pincus whose husband will go down in history as one of the greatest of this generation."

Sanger's second great achievement in her final years was to alert the world to the menace of overpopulation and the impact of an overcrowded nation on peace and maternal and child health. In no other aspect of grasping the forces of history were her ideas more original and meaningful. As early as 1922, she had written in the *Birth Control*

Review: "The greatest threat to the peace of the world is to be found in the teeming populations of Asia."

This was a tragically accurate forecast. Almost no one had made the connection between dangerously expanding populations and a country's shortage of food and natural resources that could bring territorial expansion and war. She shrewdly understood the demand by Japanese militarists for a soaring birthrate in tiny islands where 2,600 Japanese had to live off one square mile of arable land, a population density ten times that of the United States. In 1931, militarist ambitions incited the invasion of Manchuria. In Germany as well, the Nazi hunger for lebensraum demanded a boost in numbers from sixty to ninety million to satisfy the armed forces.

Although Sanger's concentration was on the right of the individual woman to decide the size of her family, she recognized that each birth played a part in determining the population growth and fate of all nations. This was a critical contribution to the laws that govern the progress of an idea. Except for a handful of neo-Malthusians in Britain, other birth control movements were limited to promoting contraception within their geographic boundaries. But for Sanger, population and peace were inextricably linked. Further, excessive births not only endangered the health of mothers, but also future prospects for their children.

It took many decades for the women's groups to catch up with the astuteness of Sanger's thesis. Until the 1990s, the feminists preached that a woman's access to birth control and abortion was the only thing that mattered, and that population problems only concerned academics and demographers. Eleanor Smeal, president of the Feminist Majority, would finally conclude: "Women were breaking down under endless childbearing. . . . We had to look at the total picture: How unchecked population growth demeaned the status of women and often ruined their lives." Consequently, women's groups flocked to the World Population Conference in Cairo in 1994.

That Sanger expanded an idea well beyond its expected stages of development is a tribute to her intellectual brilliance. She might well have decided that her American mission was achieved when a *Ladies Home Journal* poll in 1938 revealed that 79 percent of its readers now supported legalized birth control. The inherent dangers of selling birth control to underdeveloped nations might have put her off. Racist accusations could have tainted Sanger's efforts to restrict population growth in Asia and Africa. Similar criticisms of racism were leveled at her pushing birth control clinics as part of state public health agencies in North Carolina, South Carolina, Alabama, Georgia, and other Southern states in the late 1930s. U.S. Representative Sam Rayburn of Texas had never been an advocate of contraception, but when he heard about clinics in states with large percentages of blacks, he reportedly said, "Now you're really talking when you're getting birth control to them."

Sanger pursued her international objectives with her usual unquenchable energy and welcomed the possibility of world as well as domestic fame. Her Japanese trip of 1922 had the additional advantage of having J. Noah Slee as an escort. He had been courting her for over a year, and Dorothy Brush commented, "You could never quite catch her, and so she kept you fascinated always." Slee admitted later, "She was, and always will be, the greatest adventure of my life."

Birth control had only a few lonely supporters in Japan, primarily Baroness Shidzue Ishimoto. But Sanger's attacks on the militarists' demands for population growth brought seventy reporters to meet her ship in Tokyo harbor and an incessant round of speeches before the YWCA, the Chamber of Commerce, and other organizations. "No woman, native or foreign, has ever been so welcomed by Japanese men as Mrs. Sanger," Ishimoto concluded. Ishimoto would pay for her pioneering in 1937 when her birth control clinic was closed and she was jailed for ten days for "dangerous thoughts."

Sanger's trip to the World Population Conference in Geneva in 1927 provided a welcomed stopover in England where she would vacation with Havelock Ellis and other former lovers. Slee seemingly ignored these extracurricular interests. In fact, he helped to finance Ellis's move from a shabby, London apartment to a delightful country home to honor his sixty-ninth birthday and paid the salary of Françoise Cyon so that she could give up her teaching and care for Ellis at the new house. The conference boasted such distinguished attendants as Julian Huxley and Dr. William Welch of Johns Hopkins University, the dean of U.S. public health. It was the first time the international press had given serious attention to population growth. Calling the conference "an intellectual treat," the *Manchester Guardian* insisted, "It is high time the world took stock of its position."

If she had taken too many detours in the management of the American movement, Sanger consistently built on historical forces in her international objectives. Her next logical step was to open the Birth Control Information Center in London 1930 with delegates from seven nations, the precursor of the later International Planned Parenthood Federation. Another population conference in Zurich that summer would bring together for the first time promising enthusiasts who would soon take charge of the International.

Her Russian trip in 1934 provided little optimism. Abortion was legal and widely available at minuscule cost, but birth control was nonexistent. Already mindful of a potential war with Germany, one public health official told her, "Russia can do with twice the population she now has."

India in 1935 was a dazzling prospect. In an earlier stopover in London, she had already meet Jawaharlal Nehru, who had just been released from four years in prison for stirring demands for Indian independence. Nehru arranged for Sanger to meet his sister in Allahabad. India's population, expanding at the rate of 10 percent annually, had reached 400 million. Almost half of its children died before the age of five, and its maternal death rate was 24.5 per thousand compared with 4.5 in Britain. Ninety-seven percent of the people did not eat more than one full meal a day.

Mohandas Gandhi had invited Sanger to his home at Wardha, a tiny village in central India. She knew that Gandhi had proclaimed that "no nation can be free until its women have control over the power that is peculiarly theirs," but they debated for hours over birth control. He asked, "Why should people not be taught that it is immoral to have more than three or four children, and after they have had that number they should live separately?" Sanger insisted that this would require couples to achieve Gandhi's level of sainthood and destroy the "oneness" of marriage. Gandhi, she concluded, always equated love with lust and could never "accept sex as anything good, clean and wholesome."

Sanger's host was the All India Women's Conference. They had arranged for her to address the Obstetrical and Gynecological Congress and medical groups in eighteen cities. Many of them pledged to set up birth control clinics. Sanger was building a new movement through each stage of evolutionary principles and identifying future leaders of the International Planned Parenthood Federation. Her most valuable recruit was Lady Dhanvanthi Rama Rau, wife of prominent banker and later India's first ambassador to the United States.

It was only logical that the next stage of international progress would be a return to Japan after the horrors of World War II had begun to dissipate. Japan's birth rate had jumped from 29.4 per thousand in 1940 to 34. 3 in 1947, and its population had reached 80 million, as a result of increased births and a lower death rate brought about by the health standards of the U.S. occupation.

General Douglas MacArthur, the occupation commander, had enforced the Eugenics Protection Law of 1949, legalizing abortion for any cause. Ironically, abortion had never become an issue in Congress compared to the tumult it raised decades later, probably because anything that decreased the Japanese birthrate was considered permissible. Birth control, however, was hardly promoted despite the efforts of Ishimoto. She was now remarried and was Mrs. Kanju Kato. After spending most of the war in jail, she was now a labor leader and a Socialist member of parliament.

Although Sanger had been invited by Japan's largest newspaper, *Yomiuri Shimbun*, which had whipped up a birth control debate through frequent articles, MacArthur refused to grant her a visa. The protests of the country's minuscule Catholic church may have been a factor. But a more likely cause was that accusations of genocide could damage the general's presidential ambitions. Eleanor Roosevelt, who had avoided antagonizing her husband's Catholic support during his presidency, now spoke out for Sanger. MacArthur's removal from the Japanese command eliminated the visa problem. When Sanger's ship arrived a Yokohama harbor, a U.S. army officer on the dock described the scene as "the closest thing to a Hollywood opening night I'd ever seen out here."

Sanger toured Tokyo on a truck, speaking to crowds through its loudspeaker. Mrs. Kato had booked her for ten days of speeches throughout the country. In a whirlwind tour, Sanger educated Japan about the necessity of birth control. Japan would become a key member of the IPPF. When I interviewed Sanger at her Tucson home in 1953, she noted wryly, "I'm carrying the international around in my briefcase." From Japan in 1952, Sanger went on to Bombay where Nehru had formed the first Indian government and officially sanctioned birth control. With six member nations, the IPPF was legally chartered. Sanger and Lady Rama Rau were named honorary copresidents.

By 1955, the IPPF included fifteen nations, but its funding remained dismal. Sanger still retained her skill at tapping the wealthy. One of the visitors at Sanger's Tucson home was John D. Rockefeller, Jr. , who had ostensibly come to inspect her new Persian rug but soon made a healthy contribution. IPPF finances never became secure, however, until two former businessmen, Hugh Moore and General

William H. Draper, Jr., took on the job of population fund-raising. Moore ran full-page ads in newspapers across the country with such inflammatory headlines as "Pope Denounces Birth Control as Millions Starve." He coined the phrase, "the population bomb," which Dr. Paul R. Ehrlich made the title of his best-selling book. Moore and Draper had the contacts and skill to collect ten of their friends for dinner and raise at least a million dollars in an hour.

Draper had equal skills at the governmental level. Although he failed to convince President Dwight D. Eisenhower at first, Eisenhower would eventually call the population explosion "one of the most critical world problems of our time." Draper's White House lobbying would make John F. Kennedy the first president in office to support government funding of population programs. Congress approved only 29.2 million for family planning in 1957. By 1997, the amount had risen to $715 million (not including Medicaid) for federal and state combined.[2]

Until illness slowed her down at the end of the 1950s, Sanger's drive and judgment molded the International Planned Parenthood Federation. The message she stamped on her time was that human beings could shape their lives. She understood and could manipulate historical forces on an international scale.

She grasped world needs before almost anyone else and never let up on her obsessive commitment. She made birth control an instrument of social action on which the future of many nations may depend. Her great insight was that women's lives hinge on their yearning for biological freedom. "When the history of our civilization is written," H. G. Wells concluded, "it will be a biological history and Margaret Sanger will be its heroine."

Still, the population explosion has only been sporadically checked. World population today stands at six billion. The United Nations Population Division predicts 9.4 billion as a medium projection by the year 2050. Although the fertility rates of Western Europe are impressively low, the population growth of most nations in Africa and Asia remains frightening. There are a few bright spots with government initiatives in Botswana and Kenya. And the AIDS epidemic has stimulated the demand for condom protection as part of official contraceptive programs.[3]

India has become the most intractable problem with its population of one billion people, which may soon surpass China. Although the middle class is slowly adopting birth control, the rural areas cling to traditional large families. The critical factors have proved to be the literacy rate and equality for women, both responsible for a low birth rate in the Indian state of Kerala and in Thailand, which has 88 percent literacy.

Of the most populous developing countries, China and Vietnam are notable examples of population control. Both have Communist governments with strictly enforced policies that combine easy access to abortion as well as contraception. In China, urban family size has been cut from 3.3 to 1.4 births per family, and from 6.5 to 3.1 births in rural areas.

While Margaret Sanger unleashed the idea of population control almost single-handedly, she never lived to see the struggles of the International Planned Parenthood Federation in its difficult progress toward worldwide acceptance. But she was an integral part of wiping out the last legal obstacles in the United States. Both the Connecticut and Massachusetts legislatures had prohibited birth control in 1879. The laws remained on the books despite the "One Package" federal court decision of 1936, which allowed physicians to prescribe contraception at clinics or in their offices.

The Connecticut legislature authorized the closing of clinics in Danbury, Greenwich, New Haven, and Waterbury in 1940, and the state supreme court upheld the closures. Angrily insisting that "something certainly went wrong somewhere in the Connecticut League," Sanger demanded a new team with Estelle Griswold as executive director, Dr. C. Lee Buxton of Yale Medical School, and Fowler

Harper of Yale Law School and Katie Roraback as attorneys. But the U.S. Supreme Court dismissed their first case as too "abstract."[4]

After a long search to find willing doctors and plaintiffs, the Connecticut team opened a new clinic in New Haven. They scheduled the first patients for November 1, 1961, and announced it to the press. Again the state brought charges against clinic officials, and a state appellate court upheld their conviction. This time, however, the U.S. Supreme Court accepted the case, and in *Griswold v. Connecticut* on June 7, 1965, handed down a momentous decision that not only cleared Griswold and Buxton, but declared the 1879 Connecticut law unconstitutional by a seven to two vote.[5]

The language of the decision was sweeping. In the Supreme Court opinion, Justice William O. Douglas cited the Fourth and Fifth Amendments as "protecting against all governmental invasions of the sanctity of a man's home and the privacies of life" and stressed the "zone of privacy created by several constitutional guarantees." In a concurring opinion, other justices delineated "certain rights" not to be "construed to deny or discourage others retained by the people."

Already seriously ill, Sanger had been placed by her family in a convalescent home. But in periods of consciousness, she grasped the momentousness of the Supreme Court decision, which friends explained to her, and relished the final triumph of the movement (the Massachusetts law was also revoked) that had sprung from the idea of women's emancipation she had launched with *The Woman Rebel* in 1914. She died on September 6, 1966, a few days short of her eighty-eighth birthday.

Sanger died at the start of a new phase of the women's movement—securing the right to a safe abortion. In the spring of 1966, my book *Abortion*, the first social and legal analysis of the subject, was published. The sweeping language of *Griswold v. Connecticut* not only removed the last blocks to birth control, but helped to produce *Roe v. Wade* and open up a vast panoply of new rights to American women.

Chapter 6

ABORTION: FROM IDEA
TO REVOLUTION IN SEVEN YEARS

The need for abortion to end the agony of an unwanted pregnancy was rooted deep in the consciousness of American women. For more than a hundred years, women had suffered in silence until their demands erupted into a public outcry in California in 1965. Lana Phelan had been forced into a first marriage at fourteen by family pressure and quickly gave birth to a daughter. Pregnant again, she begged her doctor for help and was treated, she recalled, "like a common criminal" by a man who ordered her to "stay away from your husband." Patricia Maginnis, who had already gone through a crude Mexican abortion, saw the "brutality of the system" as a member of the Women's Army Corps in World War II. She would never forget "a soldier's wife held captive like an animal in the hospital ward, literally forced by the staff to continue a pregnancy she hated."

These two women finally revolted against laws in every state that made women criminals if they sought to make a highly personal decision about their own childbearing. They handed out leaflets on San Francisco streets, branding these laws "slavery in its cruelest sense." They referred women for abortion to Mexican doctors. They taught classes in a method of self-abortion. They were arrested in San Mateo County and jailed for eighteen hours without bail. They harnessed their anger and the anger of women everywhere by founding the Society for Humane Abortion.

The idea that abortion was a constitutional right of women produced one of the most sweeping social revolutions of the twentieth century. Its concept went far beyond birth control, which prevented a pregnancy before it started, before sperm had fertilized an egg. Abortion dealt with a developing fetus at eight or twelve weeks of gestation and occasionally longer. It raised a furious conflict between those who believed that the fetus represented only potential life and those who considered it a person from the moment of conception. It became a struggle between those convinced that a woman must control her own body and must not be made by society to bear a child against her will and those who claimed the fetus had the same rights as the mother and could not be denied the right to be born. In the endless bitterness of this religious and philosophic clash, one startling aspect has often been overlooked: that it took only seven years from the idea of legalizing abortion to its legalization nationwide through the U.S. Supreme Court's *Roe v. Wade* decision in 1973.

The remarkable speed with which this idea developed must be attributed to the special historical forces behind it. By contrast, birth control took at least thirty years for public and legal acceptance. Yet, birth control did show women they had the capacity to change their lives, and this realization empowered them to demand abortion rights and make it an obtainable objective.

In legal terms, there was the precedent of the U.S. Supreme Court *Griswold v. Connecticut* decision in 1965. Admittedly, it applied only to birth control. But its language was so broad as I had predicted, that it eventually might be pushed to encompass abortion. In the Court's seven-to-two opinion, Justice William O. Douglas established "a right to privacy, no less important than any other right carefully reserved to the people."

No historical forces were more important to abortion than the turbulent progress of the civil rights movement and the women's rights movement of the 1960s. The bloody struggle for black equality in education, the franchise, and all democratic privileges, followed soon after by the founding of the National Organization for Women and the feminist rebellion against a subservient status, bolstered the principle that individuals could come together to shape their own destinies. In few other instances has timing been more critical in the emergence of an idea . If the abortion rights campaign had started five yeas earlier, it would probably have been lost in a void.

Technology, as well, contributed to timing. Abortion had always suffered from the disadvantage of surgery as the sole technique and the frequency of infection afterward. Now the simple and efficient vacuum technique had been developed, and powerful antibiotics virtually eliminated infection. The dangers of abortion could no longer be used as an argument against its acceptance.

The strategy of the abortion rights movement determined its rapid development. Was this strategy better than previous movements? Did it develop new approaches and shrewder organizing than had ever been used before? These issues must be analyzed if we are to understand why the movement erupted so suddenly in 1965.

Abortion was hardly a new idea; in fact, the earliest known record of abortion goes back three thousand years before Christ. The Greek city-states made abortion the foundation of a well-ordered policy. In more modern times, English common law did not make abortion a crime until "the infant is able to stir in the mother's womb." English common law became the basis of U.S. laws. This policy was not changed until the 1860s and after U.S. state legislatures criminalized abortion, primarily pressured by moral fanatics like Anthony Comstock, by national needs for an expanding population to fill the country's huge open spaces, and by the medical profession, which considered rudimentary abortion methods a menace to women's health.[1]

While U.S. abortion was banned for a hundred years and confined to the darkest corners of fear and mythology, an estimated 200,000 to 1,200,000 women annually desperately sought help from backstreet practitioners, and many died or were maimed. Only a few people protested this horrific system—an occasional doctor, judge, or social reformer. None had the skill or commitment to push an idea beyond an article or speech into creative organizing.[2]

Here we come to the mysterious process of how an idea originates under different circumstances and why it leaps from theory to politics and social war. Phelan and Maginnis were obviously spurred by their own terrifying experiences with illegal abortion and those of women they knew. In my own case, I started as a writer, and the influences that soon made me a militant have to be explored. I started my book *Abortion* in 1962 and never heard of Phelan and Maginnis till 1965. It was a confluence of historical forces that brought us together on similar objectives.

Working with Margaret Sanger on her biography from 1952 to 1955, I became totally absorbed by her teachings that women could only control their childbearing and their lives through contraception. What of abortion? Although Sanger knew almost nothing about it, and I had had no personal need for it in my first marriage or succeeding friendships, the idea haunted me. The New York Academy of Medicine produced a few medical papers from Eastern Europe and Japan where abortion was legal. Except for a collection of essays that made no demand for legalized abortion, the handful of books were by retired abortionists who had done no research into the medical or social background of the subject.

It seemed absurd that punitive laws had frightened publishers away from a critique of an antiquated system. My own motivation was to correct this blight on women's freedom. Someone had to untangle this irrational record. Someone had to speak out: the responsibility seemed to be mine. First, I had spent hard months thinking through my beliefs and deciding that only the total right of abortion was the answer. Then I had to search for a publisher who could handle the risks and buck up the courage to be linked to a subject that could endanger my writing career.

Amazingly, the *New York Times Magazine* published an article I drew from the book, and the *Reader's Digest* carried a condensation, which resulted in numerous requests for help from women. I sent them to doctors doing abortions secretly. At the opening press conference for the book, a reporter asked if these referrals broke the law. Possibly, I said, but I insisted that the courts would eventually support us. By 1966, I was immersed in a movement.

The first stage of advancing an idea was coalition building. Wherever Maginnis, Phelan, and I went to speak, clusters of women wanted to know how to organize local chapters. Soon we had organizations in Chicago, Wisconsin, New York, and a dozen other states. We made sure that names and addresses were constantly exchanged so that a permanent network began to form. These local chapters would later become the sponsors of abortion rights legislation.

The next stage was a risky but carefully deliberated strategy of confrontation. Others joined me in referring women to secret doctors. The press was always informed. It not only kept abortion in the headlines, but made women realize that something was being done to secure their rights and that a movement was gathering strength.

The weight of carrying these referrals was suddenly lessened when Reverend Howard Moody of Judson Memorial Church, Reverend Finley Schaef of Washington Square Methodist Church, and other ministers and rabbis in New York City offered to set up a Clergy Consultation Service. Ostensibly, they were only advising women on the religious and moral problems of abortion. But the names of secret doctors in Louisiana, Puerto Rico and elsewhere were somehow made available. The New York model inspired clergy across the country, and soon there were at least a dozen groups in operation.

Referrals by the clergy, as we had expected, became a particular challenge to local police as the strategy of confrontation became a nationwide phenomenon and had to be crushed. Reverend Robert Hare was indicted in Middlesex County, Massachusetts, on the charge of aiding and abetting criminal abortion. In January 1970, police broke down a door panel of the office of Rabbi Max Ticktin of Chicago and seized many of his files on an arrest warrant issued by the District Court of Oakland, Michigan. Reverend Robert Wallace of Michigan warned: "You will have to jail every rabbi in Oakland County, every Unitarian cleric, at least half of the Protestant clergy and even a few Catholic priests."

Confrontations reached a violent stage in February 1969 as a *New York Times* headline announced: "Women Break Up Abortion Hearing." When a committee of the state legislature held a public forum in Manhattan, with a panel of eight male members, women swarmed into the hearing room shouting: "Men don't get pregnant. Now let's hear from the real experts—the women ." The tumult became so loud that the state senator, chairing the panel, moved the hearing to another hall and posted guards at the door to keep out the public.

Anger had become a key element. At a public meeting in March 1969 organized by the Red Stockings, a woman's liberation affiliate, scores of women stood up at New York's Washington Square Methodist Church and told about their abortions. They described their frightening search for back-alley doctors. They described their degradation and their physical and mental pain. They gave their names and the circumstances of their unwanted pregnancies. It was the first time women had made their personal tragedies a public document.

By 1967, the idea of abortion rights had stirred such public debate that it swept to the next stage of state legislative politics. There was no national organization to lay out strategy yet. A few of us who were often consulted were uncertain of what course to take. We wanted legislation that would completely repeal the old, punitive laws, but we knew we lacked a mass base in any state. Ruth Steel, a veteran of family planning in Colorado, wanted to try the American Law Institute (ALI) model of legislation. Assemblyman Richard Lamm (later elected governor) was determine to get it passed, and he did with remarkable speed. It was the first time that a state had modified the total criminalization of abortion, followed soon after by North Carolina and California.

These ALI laws were, of course, only a small step. A woman had to apply to a medical committee. Only a few thousand in each state were approved, a minuscule part of the demand. But at least it started a building process that let women know that legislators could be influenced, and it gave us experience in lobbying and made us friends among officeholders who might become allies later when we were ready for the big push. The early pioneers were committed to a strategy of all or nothing, but we were pliable enough to know that historical forces were never immutable and often had to be treated with common sense.

Should we concentrate on legislation or turn to the courts for possibly quicker progress? That was the critical debate that now enveloped us. Birth control had depended completely on the courts when Margaret Sanger failed to get anywhere with Congress. We decided that neither stage should exclude the other and that both should be worked in conjunction.

As far back as 1966, an ad hoc committee of the New York Civil Liberties Union, prominent lawyers, and I had met in New York to consider the possibilities of a judicial test case. If we could get a well-known obstetrician-gynecologist to perform an abortion openly at his hospital and then notify the district attorney, we might provoke a direct challenge to the New York state law through the courts. The project failed because we could never enlist the right doctor.

In May 1968, the arrest of Dr. Milan Vuitch in Washington, D.C., to whom I had referred many women, offered a remarkable opportunity. Vuitch courageously mixed his abortion cases with regular practice. From my study of all state laws, it especially struck me that the Washington law allowed abortion for the preservation of the woman's health as well as her life. Perhaps we could force the courts to define the exact meaning of health. Consequently, I asked Vuitch to keep careful records on every abortion patient and every physical and emotional symptom that could bolster the diagnosis of health.

Testifying before the federal court on the case that brought his arrest, Vuitch stated: "This woman had described her mental suffering—her husband's frequent desertions and extramarital affairs, and unwanted pregnancy by a husband she detested—it was all down on my chart. Only I, as her doctor, could decide whether her health had been threatened."

Vuitch's lawyers attacked the constitutionality of the Washington law under the First, Fourth, Fifth, and Ninth Amendments, stressing the precedent of the 1965 *Griswold* decision, which already protected a woman's right of privacy in the use of birth control. They also attacked the vagueness of the law and the difficulty for a doctor to define the meaning of "health."

On November 10, 1969, Judge Gerhard Gesell in the U.S. District Court declared the Washington law unconstitutional on the basis that a "woman's liberty and right of privacy extends to family, marriage, and sex matters," and that medical services must be available to the poor as well as the rich. It was the first time a federal court had overthrown an abortion law. Any licensed physician could now perform abortion legally in a Washington hospital or clinic.[3]

The movement's strategy had been shrewd. After limited progress in passing all laws in state legislatures, we were approaching the final stage of the evolutionary process by pushing hard in the courts and would now bring similar cases in other states in our quest for a climactic decision in the U.S. Supreme Court. There were practical rewards as well. We could now encourage the opening of other Washington clinics as a legal outlet for East Coast women.

A more restricted breakthrough had already been gained in Massachusetts by Bill Baird, the tough, irreverent director of a family planning clinic on Long Island. In a speech to 1,500 Boston University students in May 1967, Baird had distributed packages of contraceptive foam and read the names and addresses of Tokyo abortion clinics. He was arrested under the so-called Crimes Against Chastity law and convicted in a lower court. But on appeal, the state's supreme judicial court upheld Baird's right of free speech, which presumably meant that the names of abortion providers could now be given to women.

The progress of an idea toward its legal confirmation in the social structure had now passed well beyond the tumult of early radicalism. A mass base had been enlarged both through state chapters and the decision of the National Organization for Women to make abortion rights a fundamental plank. Still, there was little support from the establishment, from groups at the center of political and social influence. Except for the American Baptist Convention and the Unitarian-Universalist church, no major religious bodies had committed to abortion rights. In medicine, only the American Public Health Association had taken a stand; in the legal profession, only the American Civil Liberties Union. The huge network of Planned Parenthood Federation clinics and chapters remained on the sidelines except for its outspoken medical committee under Dr. Alan Guttmacher.

At this point, a small group met at my apartment in New York and decided it was essential the movement gain the cohesiveness and status of a national organization by pulling together all disparate elements. The four of us—Dr. Lonny Myers of Chicago and Reverend Don Shaw, an Episcopal canon, who had both put together an impressive Illinois chapter; Ruth P. Smith, who had been director of the Association for the Study of Abortion in New York and quit because of its refusal to adopt a political platform; and myself—decided to invite hundreds of delegates to a meeting in Chicago from February 14 to 16, 1969. This group would eventually form the National Association for Repeal of Abortion Laws or NARAL (later known as the National Abortion Rights Action League).

At least 350 delegates gathered at the Drake Hotel. We had almost no budget. Except for Betty Friedan, president of NOW, Dr. Lester Breslow, president of the American Public Health Association, and Percy Sutton, the first black borough president of Manhattan, we had no speakers of national prominence. No press photographers covered us, and signaling our lack of grasp of the meeting's significance, we had hired no official photographer. Consequently, no photograph exists of a momentous event in the origins of a social revolution.

In a turning point at the meeting, and what undoubtedly became a turning point in the surge of forces that would define the progress of an idea for the country, we debated the central issue: Would we simply focus on ALI laws in state legislatures that might take decades to bring abortion to a handful of women? Or would we take the great leap and go totally for the repeal of antiabortion laws with no compromises? The all-out position won by approximately 70 percent of the vote. We may have raced ahead of public opinion, but we were convinced it was the only position that would inflame the women's movement and the country as a whole.

After selecting a steering committee that would prepare for the election of a national board and officers, NARAL became legally and officially a nonprofit organization that fall. U.S. Representative Shirley Chisholm and former U.S. Senator Maurine Neuberger agreed to be honorary officers. New York City councilwoman Carol Greitzer was elected president, and I was elected chair of the executive committee.

The most immediate decision that would advance the movement to the final stage of electoral politics was to concentrate on New York. It could be said that no other social revolution had studied and picked its opening more carefully. After years of skirmishing over desultory ALI bills, two outstanding legislators now agreed to campaign for an all-out repeal bill. Constance Cook, an upstate Republican and chair of the Assembly's Education Committee, had already convinced Governor Nelson Rockefeller to sign any progressive act passed by the legislature. Her cosponsors were Franz Leichter, a veteran reform Democrat from Manhattan who had lined up most of the New York City bloc, and Assembly Speaker Stanley Steingut from Brooklyn.

Few campaigns had ever been put together with such exhaustive detail. We had religious committees, including the Protestant State Council of Churches and the American Jewish Congress working in every district. We had NOW, the National Association of Social Workers, housing groups, student groups, and consumer groups. Voter pressure through telegrams enveloped swing legislators. A Syracuse women's group collected two thousand signatures on a petition to get Assemblyman Kenneth Bartlett's support. Assembly Speaker Perry Durea in conservative Suffolk County was persuaded to back the bill. State Senators Norman Lent and Edward Speno, Republicans in Republican-dominated Nassau County, switched from opposition to the repeal position.

Over the whole campaign loomed the powerful influence of the Catholic hierarchy. On March 29, 1970, a pastoral letter was read in every Catholic Church urging parishioners to make their legislators oppose the bill. Three Catholic assemblymen switched against us. One holdout in the Bronx was bombarded with calls from priests calling him a "murderer."

When the senate took up the bill, Basil Paterson, a black Catholic from Harlem, announced his independence from the church. The Senate bill, removing abortion completely from the criminal code, got thirty-one votes with only twenty-nine needed for passage. In the assembly, however, Cook was still fighting for every vote. Black legislators buttonholed Arthur Eve of Buffalo and stressed the importance of abortion to low-income blacks. At the final roll call, he switched from no to yes one of four crucial votes.

The assembly bill was still bottled up in the Codes Committee, and Cook was convinced she couldn't get it out unless the right of abortion was limited to twenty-four weeks of pregnancy. She called the NARAL executive committee desperately over the weekend for its agreement. Only a handful of cases after that time limit would be affected, and with this landmark legislation at stake, NARAL agreed.

On April 9, Cook called the bill from the table and at 4:30 P.M., the tally started. With the balcony crowded with our campaign teams tensely totaling up the votes, and opponents around us shouting "murder" with every yes vote, it was soon apparent that we would lose in a seventy-four to seventy-four tie. It was a moment of immeasurable desperation

Seconds before the Speaker would announce our defeat, George Michaels, a Democrat from upstate Auburn, rose from his seat. In a faltering voice, his face drained of color, he talked of his three sons in a devout Jewish family. "My own sons called me a whore for voting against this bill," he said. He had spent thirty-seven months in the Marines in World War II, much of it in Pacific combat, but this decision "was worse than anything."

As the Assembly Hall turned to chaos, he switched his vote. With the Speaker also voting yes, he mumbled, sobbing, "What's the use of getting elected if you don't stand for something?" An unknown legislator had been catapulted into history. The senate quickly passed the same bill, and Governor Rockefeller signed it into law, effective July 1, 1970.

Only a year after the founding of NARAL, the movement had reached its final stages. Passage of a sweeping abortion rights bill in a bellwether state eased the way for similar bills in other states. It meant that patients could now come from the Eastern seaboard and Midwest for treatment. It meant that the balance between legislation and courts was the correct route to evolutionary progress, and that we could now concentrate on moving judicial test cases toward the U.S. Supreme Court.

Chapter 7

WE RODE THE CREST: BUILDING THE MASS BASE IN ABORTION RIGHTS

"The momentum of the groundswell," Dr. Patricia Steinhoff of the University of Hawaii called the forces behind the Hawaiian legislation. The bill fell slightly short of the standards set in New York, legalizing abortion in hospitals during the first twenty-four weeks of pregnancy and requiring a ninety-day residency. But it was a remarkable example of how the movement had learned to harness the lobbying strength of a broad spectrum of groups and exploit the momentum already gained by earlier court decisions and the New York campaign.

Joan Hayes, legislative chairperson of the American Association of University Women, invited more than one hundred organizations to a citizens seminar on abortion. The coalition that sprung from it included not just committed women in the National Association of Social Workers and the Council of Churches but also drew on groups never involved in abortion before, such as the International Longshore Workers and other unions in the AFL-CIO and even the chamber of commerce. There was a student march and a petition drive on campuses.

Recruiting the University of Hawaii's School of Public Health to prepare a questionnaire, Hayes sent it to physicians on the islands most concerned with abortion. Almost every obstetrician-gynecologist and 80 percent of psychiatrists supported a sweeping abortion rights bill. With polls showing 90 percent of readers of the two principal newspapers, the *Star Bulletin* and the *Advertiser*, backing such a bill, Hayes concentrated on the legislature in mid-1969.

Her particular target was State Senator Vincent Yano. Although a Catholic, he had long opposed government intrusion into matters of conscience. Equally important, he was chairperson of the committee on public health, welfare, and housing, which would introduce the bill. The coalition flooded legislators with the results of the doctors' questionnaire and sent teams to lobby every legislator at the capitol. On September 10, 1969, Yano announced he would back the bill, and his committee was leaning toward his position.

In a last effort to block the bill, Bishop John Scanlan, the Knights of Columbus, and other Catholic dignitaries failed to halt the momentum that Hayes and the coalition had stirred in the legislature. In late February 1970, the house approved the abortion rights bill 31 to 20, the senate by 15 to 9. Governor John A. Burns, a Catholic who, like Yano, considered abortion a matter of individual conscience, let the bill become law on March 13 without signing it.

In Alaska, where a strong abortion rights bill was also embroiled in legislative debate in 1970, Helen Nienhueser, chairperson of the Alliance for Humane Abortion, analyzed the historical forces: "We rode the crest of something I still can't define—but that something was clearly changing attitudes on the part of the American public, assisted by coverage of the basic issues in magazines and newspapers."

The bill had been sponsored by State Senator John Rader of Anchorage. But it was the alliance that wangled the media coverage and built an idea into a public demand for radical change. Like New York and Hawaii, the strategy depended on local campaigns. The State Nurses Association, the Commission on the Status of Women, and other groups provided the first recruits. But it was Jan Erickson, Evey Ruskin, and the alliance's hard core of fifty who launched the petition drives and telephone and letter chains to convert each legislator. Each of the fifty gave regular coffee parties for his or her friends.

Each attendant was persuaded to give his or her own parties. The Alaska Council of Churches joined in. Students concentrated on polling, and Anchorage Community College study found that 85 percent favored the strongest possible bill.

Senator Rader, a graduate of the University of Kansas Law School, had lived in Alaska since 1951 with his wife and three children. His family physician was Dr. Rodman Wilson, an officer of the State Medical Association. Both agreed that abortion should become purely a medical choice between a woman and her doctor, and Wilson put this belief into a resolution that passed the medical association. Except for New York, the most progressive medical groups had grown up in the two newest states. Significantly, the movement was taking advantage of those areas where the forces behind abortion rights were strongest and quick breakthroughs were likely.

When Rader introduced his first bill to allow free choice in the first twenty weeks of pregnancy, he could not persuade a single senator to cosponsor it with him. Then Nienhueser's alliance began its campaign, and Rader admitted he had "grossly underestimated" the groundswell the women stirred. On March 4, 1970, he made his first test in the senate, but secured only ten votes of eleven needed for passage. After the Hawaii bill passed, Rader submitted a duplicate that covered twenty-four weeks of pregnancy (with no in-hospital or residency provisions). It went to the floor on April 1, 1970.

The crucial vote was a new member, Senator Kay Poland of Kodiak, a Catholic. When another Catholic attacked her support of the bill in an angry debate, she retorted: "I am a Catholic. I am adopted. I am, of course, a woman,. I don't feel I can sit here and make a decision for my fellow women."

Rader's bill passed by a vote of 13 to 7. On April 9, 1970, the house approved it 29 to 10. The momentary celebration collapsed a week later when Governor Keith Miller, a Methodist married to a Catholic, vetoed the bill. Rader and the alliance worked feverishly to rally the two-thirds, or 40 votes, needed for an override. On April 30, both houses stood firm. The veto was overturned 41 to 17 with 1 vote to spare.

NARAL, which essentially represented the movement, never dominated state groups. But it tried to measure where historic forces were strongest and put its limited money where it could make a difference. NARAL wanted a new law on the West Coast. Dr. Samuel Goldenberg, a NARAL board member, urged Washington state as the next test. The Seattle Radical Women demonstrated at Olympia in March 1969 and "blasted the abortion bill into a high priority item." They proclaimed: "We refuse to be considered criminals." This would be the start of the bitterest campaign yet.

The Catholic hierarchy had decided to make Washington its best-financed and organized battleground. Lorenzo Milam, a *Seattle Post-Intelligence* columnist, attacked the "seven Catholics who help run our state from the comfort and power of the Senate Rules Committee in Olympia . . . two more who are married to Catholics, and a handful of others who quiver every time they get a call from the local representative of El Papa (the Pope)." Catholic churches threatened to boycott the paper. Milam refused to retract; he then left or was fired.

Abortion Action Now, a feminist coalition, gathered two thousand people at the capitol in late March. A police lieutenant tried to stop a delegation from entering the capitol until the state attorney general approved their admission. "The idea that poor and working women would make such a vociferous and angry demand on the august real estate dealers, lawyers, and petty businessmen, who run the state's government, was stunning to the all-male Senate," complained the Seattle Radical Women's newsletter.

As the public groundswell mounted, the Rules Committee finally let the abortion rights bill reach the floor. Dean Dorothy Strawn of the University of Washington commented, "I'm seeing agreement from people of all ages and races, income groups and political viewpoint." The Senate passed the bill on January 30, 1970; the house a few days later. It was hardly an ideal bill, allowing abortion the first seventeen weeks of pregnancy and requiring a husband's consent if living with his wife and a ninety-day residency. The bill also required a popular referendum for approval and would galvanize the state for nine months.

The Catholic Church's political fronts poured huge sums into billboards, media, and leaflets that accused doctors and clergy of fostering "murder." The line between church and state disintegrated: The house's minority leader addressed a forum in May to train priests on tactics for defeating the bill. The women's coalition deplored the Catholic Church's "arrogance and presumption" and insisted "we won't be chattels anymore."

On November 1, 1970, the electorate approved the abortion bill by the convincing margin of 56 to 44 percent. "A grand defeat for sexists and reactionaries," the *University of Washington Daily* proclaimed. Combined with the California Supreme Court decision of September 5, 1969, which declared the state's antiabortion law unconstitutional after a challenge by Dr. Leon Belous, the movement now had two abortion rights centers on the West Coast. The Reverend Hugh Anwyl, a NARAL board member and head of the local Clergy Consultation Service, was soon processing cases in less than two days. By 1972, California was doing 135,000 legal abortions a year, the second highest total of any state behind New York.

The speed with which historic forces had been grasped and exploited at this early stage was a testament to the movement's consensual approach. Of course, Planned Parenthood's success had paved the way. But in contrast to its domination by Margaret Sanger and little grassroots organizing, the decisions in abortion rights were hammered out by NARAL's executive committee in collaboration with state and local chapters. There were occasional mistakes: NARAL supported a public referendum to overthrow the old Michigan law, not realizing that the Catholic hierarchy would throw about half a million dollars in media spots and billboards against it. The referendum was badly defeated in 1972.

The Midwest had to be opened up. NARAL decided to use legal tests by individual doctors and clinics as its strategy. Referring to thousands of indigent women applying for abortion, Dr. Edgar Keemer, NARAL's Midwest vice president and a veteran Detroit physician, insisted, "The Detroit Medical Society must not sit on its professional posterior while dollar discrimination stalks the ghetto like Bull Connor's dogs." Deciding on confrontation and risking arrest and the loss of his license, Keemer publicly announced that he had done an abortion on a forty-year-old welfare mother of seven who had given up the pill because of side effects. Significantly, the district attorney brought no charges, and Keemer kept on doing abortions for indigent patients. Medicaid even gave its stamp of approval by paying for each patient.

This strategy was carried to Wisconsin where Anne Gaylor, a NARAL board member, confronted the state assembly with the case of an indigent woman who had jabbed a coat hanger into her uterus and was rushed to a hospital. "It is a terrible thing to watch a young girl die, and to know that her death was unnecessary, a total waste," a clergy service member stated.

Working with Gaylor, Dr. Alfred Kennan of the University of Wisconsin Medical School opened the state's first, freestanding abortion clinic on February 1, 1971. He was soon taking one hundred cases a week, and the police arrested Kennan and his staff. But when NARAL when to court and got a restraining order, the clinic reopened in May.

Convinced that the strategy of confrontation would carry the movement to the next stage of success, NARAL board member Dr. Robert M. Livingston announced that he would start doing abortions in his New Jersey office. "It's time we stopped the nonsense and the charade and the debasing practice of making women who do not want to continue their pregnancies drive way out of state for something they should have legal access to here," Livingston stated. Despite a federal court ruling that the New Jersey law was unconstitutional, the state district attorney warned Livingston he was "susceptible to arrest." He kept doing abortions and was never arrested.

An essential part of NARAL's progress was not just winning in the courts and state legislatures but making the new laws work. The real test came in New York after passage of the landmark 1970 bill. In addition to the responsibility of handling a flood of patients from the East Coast and Midwest, NARAL had to grapple with the bureaucracy. The state health commissioner immediately tried to restrict abortions to hospitals and hospital clinics, which would not only raise costs but lead to long waiting lists.

On July 1, 1970, the day the New York law went into effect, NARAL held a conference to train doctors from across the state in abortion techniques. At a NARAL press conference, headlined by the *New York Times* with "Physicians Urged to Defy City and State Guidelines on Abortion," I urged doctors to set up their own freestanding clinics with a price limit of $300. By August, when city hospitals had only done a few thousand abortions and had a huge backlog, NARAL pickets marched in front of hospitals with signs that read, "Raped by the Medical Bureaucracy." To intensify the pressure, Reverend Howard Moody of the Clergy Consultation Service raised the money to open a large clinic in Manhattan with a top price of $200.

Whether it was NARAL's political lobbying or simply a governmental revamping, New York City now established a superagency, the Health Services Administration. Its new director, Gordon Chase, immediately approved abortion at any freestanding clinic that had a qualified laboratory and blood plasma and was near a backup hospital in case of emergency.

Moody's clinic was so swamped with patients that he moved to an enlarged space on East 62nd Street with a staff of thirty part-time obstetricians and a price of only $125. The next few months proved that a freestanding clinic could achieve the highest medical standards. There were no deaths in the first 26,000 cases. Uterine perforations were just 1.4 per 1,000 cases. Bungled abortions—the blight of the prelegal era—virtually disappeared.

One of the immutable laws in the historic progress of an idea is that social forces are soon met by counterforces. Successful in defeating the Michigan referendum, the Catholic hierarchy began to chip away at the New York state law, particularly in Westchester County and on Long Island, where Catholic officials pushed through local ordinances prohibiting or limiting freestanding clinics. This trend was stopped June 1, 1972, when the state court of appeals ruled that local governments could not interfere with the practice of medicine, including abortion.

The Catholic counterattack would reach a crescendo when Cardinal Terence Cooke vowed to overturn the New York law and declared April 16, 1972, "Right to Life Sunday." A thousand people, mainly parochial schoolchildren, marched down Manhattan's Fifth Avenue. Buses carried thousands more to Albany the next day. Their lobbying was beginning to wear down Catholic legislators who had voted for the bill two years before. The Catholic Church secured enough switches to revoke the 1970 law, and everything now depended on Governor Nelson Rockefeller's veto. Criticizing the "extreme of personal vilification" in recent months, the governor announced, "I do not believe it is right for one group to impose its vision of morality on an entire society." His veto was upheld by legislators, and the movement survived the first serious crisis in its dazzling progress.

Much of the power of the Catholic Church depended on its illegal use of tax-exempt religious money and facilities in political races. At Sunday Mass, for example, six churches in Westchester County, New York, opposed the reelection of R. Bradley Boal to the county legislature and produced his defeat. In Orange County, California, fourteen churches set up tables on religious property after Mass to persuade parishioners to switch their party registration and defeat a proabortion rights plank in a state bill. The most blatant example was an editorial in the San Antonio, Texas, diocesan newspaper, which ran a long list of favored candidates and taunted the government in its headline, "To the IRS—'Nuts!!'"

When the original members were rotated off the NARAL board in 1975, the majority of us formed the Abortion Rights Mobilization (ARM), and an early objective was to block these infractions of the tax law by suing the National Conference of Catholic Bishops in federal court. The evidence was indisputable, scores of examples in official Catholic media listing antiabortion candidates to support. Realizing they couldn't win at trial, the Catholic Church's lawyers challenged our plaintiffs' "standing," a complex regulation in federal courts that highly restricts the right to sue. Decision after decision came down in our favor while the church's lawyers kept appealing on the standing issue. After years of briefs and arguments, the U.S. Supreme Court finally denied ARM standing.

Still, ARM had basically accomplished its objective. The National Conference of Catholic Bishops would order all dioceses that no church money or facilities could henceforth be used in political campaigns. The lawbreaking would now come from the Protestant fundamentalists. A few small churches were blocked from political activity, but the principal case brought by the Federal Elections Commission against Pat Robertson's Christian Coalition produced only limited results. Interpreting the election law narrowly, a federal judge in 1999 ruled that the coalition's voter guides and scorecards did not amount to "express advocacy" of Republican candidates. The judge, however, did find the coalition guilty of endorsing former House Speaker Newt Gingrich and providing mailing lists to Senate candidate Oliver North.

Despite the seemingly unstoppable forces behind the abortion rights movement, the year 1972 brought a time of reckoning. The passage of strong, state legislation came to a halt. Bills were defeated in Connecticut and Florida. We obviously lacked the workers and money to launch campaigns in state after state, Michigan being the prime example of overconfidence. Historical forces must be analyzed carefully, new pressures applied to the most propitious openings. The NARAL executive committee now decided the opening lay in the federal courts.

Following the influential *Griswold* case in Connecticut in 1965, Bill Baird's arrest for distributing contraceptives to Boston University students came before the U.S. Supreme Court in 1972. The ninety-three-year-old Massachusetts law forbade giving or selling birth control to unmarried women. The majority decision, delivered by Justice William J. Brennan, the only Catholic on the Court, was even more sweeping in its wording than *Griswold*. "If the right of privacy means anything," the court ruled, "it is the right of the individual, married or single, to be free from unwarranted intrusion into matters so fundamentally affecting a person as the decision whether to bear or beget a child." Again it seemed that this wording could eventually be applied to abortion as well as birth control.

Who can predict the rumblings of society that may affect the Supreme Court? Certainly the actions of crucial national organizations must be considered a factor. The American Medical Association's House of Delegates had already approved in-hospital abortion with two-doctor consent. The American College of Obstetrics and Gynecology approved abortion with only one doctor consenting. The American Bar Association voted approval in the first twenty weeks of pregnancy.

Just as they did in the *Brown* decision on public schools, the justices must have taken notice of changing social attitudes. As a result of landmark legislation in New York, Hawaii, Alaska, and other states and judicial opinions nationwide, at least 600,000 legal abortions were already being performed (and probably many more unrecorded). Legal abortion was virtually a *fait accompli*. A Gallup poll in 1972 showed that 64 percent of respondents (including a remarkable 56 percent of Catholics) agreed that the "decision to have an abortion should be made by a woman and her physician."

There was a momentum that had to be recognized. A cluster of cases, including a New Jersey case recognizing the "right of privacy cognizable under the Ninth and Fourteenth Amendments," were headed toward the Supreme Court. But the fastest moving were *Roe v. Wade* in Texas and *Doe v. Bolton* in Georgia. *Roe* attacked the old laws throughout much of the country which only allowed abortion to save the life of the mother. *Doe* attacked a few "therapeutic" laws passed in 1967, allowing abortion for a handful of women with medical committee approval.[1]

The Supreme Court heard arguments on both cases on December 13, 1971, but there were only seven justices on the bench, and the court ordered a rehearing when President Nixon's two latest appointments were seated. Meanwhile, the movement's legal expertise concentrated on preparing the trial lawyers. Margie Pitts Hames, a graduate of Vanderbilt Law School in 1961, would carry the Georgia pleadings. But in Texas, Sarah Weddington had only graduated from University of Texas Law School in 1967. The veteran lawyers who worked with them on court tactics were Professor Cyril Means of New York Law School, chairperson of NARAL's legal committee; Roy Lucas, prior chairperson of NARAL's legal committee; Harriet Pilpel, attorney for the Planned Parenthood Federation; and Norman Dorsen of the ACLU.

Despite some quibbling over credit and which lawyers would argue in court—quickly settled by the advisory team—there had been surprisingly few errors in the movement's rapid progress. The selection of the Texas plaintiff, known as Roe but later identified as Norma McCorvey, was disturbingly sloppy. No one had checked her background, which included drug-taking and other liabilities. Fortunately, the opposing Texas officials had made no check either, and

McCorvey's record never tainted the arguments. Although McCorvey later gloried in her role and became a star on the speaking circuit, her psychological problems and instability eventually led her to attack abortion rights, and she proved an embarrassment to the movement.

It came like a thunderclap, one of the most momentous and controversial decisions ever handed down by the U.S. Supreme Court. On January 22, 1973, in *Roe v. Wade* the Court, by a seven to two vote, abolished all the punitive state laws that had imprisoned women for more than one hundred years. Modeled largely on the 1970 New York state law, *Roe* gave women and their doctors an unimpeded choice of abortion in the first three months of pregnancy. State intervention was prohibited in the second three months of pregnancy except to regulate the appropriate medical procedure in the interest of the mother's health. After fetal viability, a state could only "proscribe" abortion "except when it is necessary to preserve the life or health of the mother."

The Court's ruling stemmed primarily from the right of privacy, which it deemed "broad enough to encompass a woman's decision whether or not to terminate her pregnancy." The privacy principle, which had been stressed by the movement in new state laws and court cases from its earliest days, had been resoundingly vindicated.

Equally critical was the Court's analysis of the "difficult question of when life begins." Rebutting the opposition's incessant claim that an incipient fetus constituted human life from the moment of conception, the Court held that "the word 'person', as used in the Fourteenth Amendment, does not include the unborn." The Court, however, never influenced right-wing Catholics or Protestant fundamentalists, who continued to insist that a person existed at conception and that abortion was "murder."

Roe v. Wade was the climactic point in the progress of an idea that had shaken the country as it had rarely been shaken before and had moved from stage to stage in only seven years. One idea had galvanized an enormous popular movement that was central to the belief that individuals could control their own destiny. At a time when too many had grown jaded with society's failure to meet their deepest needs, abortion rights invigorated the belief that radical change was attainable.

Women had dominated the development of the movement in every state. They had always recognized that there was nothing more destructive to the meaning and potential of their lives than unwanted motherhood. Now they had succeeded in overthrowing a savage system. The issue of abortion rights would build the National Organization for Women and other feminist coalitions and give them the confidence to grapple with other objectives.

Abortion rights essentially represented a struggle between the individual and authoritarianism. By gaining control of their procreation, women would henceforth challenge male authoritarianism and the religious conservatives who had made it their bastion. This clash would continue to disturb the nation. They day after *Roe* was announced, the movement's leadership celebrated over champagne. Many wanted to disband their coalitions, but a few NARAL executives insisted that a new counterattack would be coming. The prediction was accurate. Abortion would soon become the cutting edge of the conservative agenda and divide the politicians and the electorate as never before.

Chapter 8

EXPANDING THE IDEA OF ABORTION RIGHTS AGAINST COUNTERATTACK

Historical forces behind an idea must be rooted deep in society. Yet, when an unshakable minority opposes an idea, the majority must not only hold its constituency together, but develop new strategies to bolster its gains. The peculiarities of the American political system may make this difficult. It is ironic that possibly the two most revolutionary changes in U.S. history—abortion rights and the abolition of slavery—had to deal with political crises that made their tasks harder.

Although slavery was legally ended by post–Civil War constitutional amendments, African-Americans in the South made their gains entirely through the presence of federal troops. Pressure groups in the North, largely responsible for emancipation, virtually disbanded. And when the bitterly contested election of 1876 required the swing of a few electoral votes to give Rutherford B. Hayes the presidency, the Republican party bought those votes through a deal that removed troops from the South. Thereupon, the old Confederacy invented a system that reinstated the bondage of the black population.

The election of the year 2000 raised similar possibilities. Determined to wipe out *Roe v. Wade,* which legalized abortion, Bush pledged to nominate new Supreme Court justices with antiabortion leanings and to ban RU 486, the abortion pill, from the country.

The circumstances were remarkably similar to Hayes. Bush achieved the White House with Florida's electoral votes. As complications of the state tally became even more tangled than in 1876, the Supreme Court gave Bush the presidency by a five to four vote in an astonishingly murky decision. Bush's legitimacy remained doubtful not only because he lost the popular vote by a large margin, but because a careful recount of the Florida vote by a consortium of prestigious newspapers and accountants showed that Al Gore, the Democratic candidate, had actually won if all counties had been re-tabulated.

Yet, Bush immediately started appeasing the right-wing factions that were the base of his campaign. He restored the so-called Global Gag Rule, instituted by President Reagan in 1984 and ended by President Clinton in 1993. The gag forbids all nongovernmental organizations, such as International Planned Parenthood, from using U.S. Agency for International Development money for birth control and maternal health if they also provide counsel on abortion (even using their own money). Particularly in poor countries, this is a dangerous invasion of women's health care.[1]

The Bush policy was carried over to Congress with pending Republican bills restricting the use of RU 486. The secretary of Health and Human Services announced he would have the Food and Drug Administration (FDA) reexamine the safety of the pill.

The issue seemed ludicrous since Abortion Rights Mobilization (ARM), a New York group that I head, had already demonstrated its safety in more than nine thousand cases with FDA approval. Hundreds of thousands of cases in France, Britain, and other countries reaffirmed this conclusion.

By early 2001, abortion rights had become an issue of politics rather than medicine. The *Roe* decision clung by a slim five to four vote in the Supreme Court, and Bush's Court appointments would now hold the balance of power. The Senate, which had to approve nominations, would be decisive. With democrats now in the minority, everything depended on whether the prochoice majority could amass enough influence and ensure new justices with objective backgrounds on abortion.

Another Bush strategy made this aim more difficult. In March 2001, the White House notified the American Bar Association that it would end its longtime role in evaluating candidates for federal judgeships because of the association's "liberal" bent.

The power of an idea, guaranteed by *Roe* since 1973, had thus been shaken by the dubious results of the Florida election and Bush's dependence on the religious right. The crucial question was whether Protestant fundamentalists and conservative Catholics (estimated at 15 to 17 percent of the electorate) should be allowed to clamp their views on the rest of the country.

The religious right based its attack on moral beliefs that allowed no rebuttal. It was convinced that a person exists from the moment that the sperm meets the egg and that abortion, therefore, was "murder." Although the Supreme Court in *Roe* and lower federal courts in similar cases have ruled that no person exists until an infant has emerged from the womb, the religious right has ignored the judiciary.

Its position reflects more than morality. It goes deep into the conservative need to maintain male dominance. Once birth control and abortion emancipated women from forced childbearing, women could seek equality and better education and jobs. Abortion not only eroded the old concept of "family values," but the conviction that women must be totally subservient to men. Still, as late as 1998, the Southern Baptist Convention extolled the "servant leadership of her husband."[2]

The religious right ignored the drastic changes of recent decades that had made the previous norm of homebound wife and a least two children living together under husband domination virtually obsolete. In 1998, both spouses were employed at least part time in 51 percent of married couples with children. Fifty-nine percent of women with babies younger than a year were employed.[3]

Women were making increasing progress in education and jobs. Forty-five percent of all Ph.D. degrees were awarded them in 1996. Women made up 44 percent of lawyers and 41 percent of doctors in 1996 and 62 percent of psychologists in 1998. At universities such as Brown and UCLA, men were a minority of the student body.

Despite advances, abortion rights came under increasing attack. Seven doctors and clinic personnel have been assassinated in Atlanta, Boston, Pensacola, Florida, and Buffalo, New York, in recent years. There were 41 bombings, 141 cases of arson, and 942 incidents of vandalism in 1998.

The objective, of course, was to shut down clinics. But a corollary result was to scare off doctors from performing abortions and to diminish the participation of young doctors, often because many teaching hospitals have given up courses in abortion techniques. The disturbing consequence is that only 17 percent of the nation's counties now have abortion providers.

The number of fanatics who resort to murder in the belief they are fulfilling God's will has been abetted by the failure of the FBI and police to apprehend them. James Kopp, the prime suspect in the assassination of Dr. Barnett A. Slepian of Buffalo, took years to be deported from France to the United States for a trial. The gun used in the killing took a month to find, although hidden only a few inches below the surface of the doctor's backyard. FBI teams have searched in vain for years in North Carolina for Eric Rudolph, suspected in the Atlanta bombing. Although mainstream opponents have deplored violence, extremists have stirred enough frenzy around abortion clinics to create an atmosphere that leads to violence.

Acceptance of an idea is not enough. New approaches must be developed to motivate public support. In one approach, ARM conceived a lawsuit aimed at those using the Internet to promote murder. ARM's pro bono law firm, Paul, Weiss, Rifkind, Wharton, and Garrison, brought suit in Oregon federal court, charging that the

Army of God and similar groups had put "wanted for murder" posters on the Internet that listed names, addresses, phones, and license plate numbers of abortion providers. The names of doctors already assassinated were crossed off.[4]

ARM's suit claimed that this was a direct incitement to violence that went far beyond First Amendment protection of free speech. The federal jury agreed. On February 2, 1999, the culprits were found guilty and fined $107,000,000. The defendants have appealed.

In ARM's search to strengthen an idea, it turned to RU 486, the abortion pill developed in France. ARM's theory was that if thousands of U.S. doctors could administer RU 486 in their offices, opponents would have trouble rousing violence against such large numbers. Since RU 486 could also be taken as early as three weeks after pregnancy and caused a blood flow only a little heavier than a normal period with no fetal tissue discernible, ARM also thought that moderate opponents might consider it less objectionable than a surgical procedure.

Following my strategy of first informing the public through the media, I wrote a thorough survey of the subject in the book *RU 486*, published in 1991. We then decided on a test case that would inflame the public. Although the Republican administration had banned the pill, we found a clause in the law—allowing an individual to bring into the country an essential drug for personal use—that might provide an opening. We decided to risk it. It took months to find a few carefully guarded French pills and to locate a young, pregnant woman who could stand up under publicity. I flew to London with Leona Benten. Our staff here notified U.S. customs and other authorities we would return on July 1, 1992, to challenge the law. One of our lawyers predicted jail.[5]

At least forty TV cameras and other members of the media awaited us at JFK airport. Customs, as expected, seized the pills we carried. We opposed the seizure in federal court (a case still unresolved), but

Benten meanwhile was forced to have a surgical abortion. Still, our objective had been accomplished. Months of press had virtually made RU 486 a household name.

Our long-range purpose was to keep organizing the people behind the idea of bringing the pill to U.S. women. To learn how to manufacture it, we studied the original French patent and smuggled in pills from China to analyze their makeup. We spent months finding and equipping a secret laboratory in Westchester County, just outside New York City, and locating experts in steroids to run it. Within a year, we had made about ninety pills, the first in the United States. Since large-scale manufacturing required a commercial plant, we found, after a long search, such a plant and signed a contract. We then submitted the plant's processing to the FDA and gained approval in 1996.

By the year 2001 ARM had treated more than 9,000 women in a research project directed by Dr. Eric Schaff of the University of Rochester Medical School in fifteen nationwide outlets, including Columbia-Presbyterian and Montefiore hospitals in New York City. Our record was notable: a success rate (completed abortions) of 97 percent, higher than the European rate. We pioneered by cutting the dose from 600 milligrams (as used in other countries) to 200 milligrams with equally efficient results. The cut in dosage allowed a woman to take the booster drug at home with the comfortable support of a partner or family.[6]

To expand the potential of an idea, ARM now explored the treatment of fibroids with RU 486 in a project directed by Dr. Steven Eisinger of the University of Rochester Medical School. Fibroid tumors of the uterus plague almost 25 percent of women of childbearing age and have led to a disturbingly high rate of hysterectomies. Early tests have shown that RU 486 can wipe out or sharply shrink fibroids, but it will take a few years of research to prove that the effect of the drug is lasting and harmless. ARM next started research on the impact of RU 486 on endometriosis. The Feminist Majority Foundation had been treating cancerous brain tumors with RU 486 with optimistic results.

In contrast with the speed of ARM's projects, the Population Council of New York City, holder of the U.S. patent, stumbled for years in finding a suitable, commercial distributor until the Danco group was given the assignment. After struggling through the FDA approval process, Danco has steadily boosted sales of the pill to doctors and clinics. Still, President Bush's threats dampen its acceptance. ARM followed its usual confrontation policy by warning in newspaper ads: "No matter what limitations your administration puts on RU 486, ARM intends to keep distributing this essential drug to doctors just as we have done before."[7]

Continuing the thesis that an idea needs new approaches to enforce public confidence, the morning-after pill (approved by the FDA in 1998) represents a critical technological advance. A small, packaged version of the long-accepted, monthly schedule of birth control pills, the morning-after pill must be used within two or three days after unprotected intercourse. Almost infallibly, it eliminates the possibility of pregnancy.[8]

Since it acts before sperm has fertilized the egg, the morning-after pill would logically appeal to the religious right. It should cut down the number of abortions: no fetus has yet been formed. However, extremists cling to "abstinence only" as the sole solution and may brand the pill as a variation of birth control. "If you go according to God's law, birth control should not be legal," proclaimed Mark Wildness, a right-wing advocate in January 2000.[9]

The Reproductive Health Technologies Project, sponsor of the "emergency contraception hotline," has confronted another problem. The morning-after pill requires a doctor's prescription, and many women who need it, particularly the young and poor, cannot find medical help quickly enough to meet the time limit. So, at least sixty-five health and women's groups petitioned the FDA in February 2001 to allow the pill to be sold over the counter at drugstores. Although this system has been adopted in Britain, South Africa, and other countries, the Bush administration is not likely to support it.

In fact, an intensifying counterattack from the religious right has exploited a disturbing weakness in abortion rights, which it labeled "partial birth" abortion. This is a loaded term, of course, to describe procedures done in the last month or two of pregnancy. No one accurately knows the number of procedures done. The *New York Times* estimated "only a few hundred." A CBS story gave a figure of 600 to 1,000.[10]

In an effort to rebut the argument that women were having late abortions not for medical causes but as a last-minute whim, Tammy Watts testified before a congressional committee that the doctor described her fetus as having a "butterfly opening in the back . . . missing chambers in her heart . . . liver and kidneys failing." Another witness, Vicki Wilson, described the brain of her fetus as "growing outside its head. . . . It was actually bigger than the head."

In its counterattack, the religious right stressed the unsavory details of two procedures: injection of digitalis into the fetal heart and extraction of fetal parts; an instrument inserted into the fetal neck to suction out the brains. Congress, thereupon, passed a bill to ban late abortions, but it was worded so badly that it could criminalize many early abortions. President Clinton vetoed the bills.

Nebraska and other states passed their own bills to block late abortion. At this point, it took special courage to confront the religious right. As part of the theory that a dramatic challenge can often be pivotal to a movement's progress, Dr. Leroy Carhart of Bellevue, Nebraska, who performed late abortions and was an ARM outlet for RU 486, decided the law had to be tested. With counsel from the Center for Reproductive Law and Policy, he went to federal court. On June 28, 2000, the Supreme Court by a five to four vote declared Nebraska's law unconstitutional on the basis that it had no health exception and imposed an "undue burden" on a woman's right to choose abortion.

Another tactic aimed at eliminating abortion (and other reproductive health services) stemmed from the merger of local hospitals. As a result of depleted finances and other problems, nonsectarian hospitals are increasingly merging with Catholic hospitals, whose religious rules prohibit abortion, birth control, voluntary sterilization, and even in vitro fertilization. In New Hampshire, after the merger of Manchester's Elliot Hospital with the Catholic Medical Center, a doctor was forbidden to abort a patient who had gone into dangerously early labor, which he considered a threat to her health. She had to take an eighty-mile taxi ride to another facility. The case caused so much community controversy that the merger was ended.

At least 105 similar mergers have occurred since 1995. Occasionally a compromise is worked out, establishing a separate clinic nearby for abortion. But the more likely result is that all reproductive health services in the area are terminated.

"Merger mania" has brought increasing community resistance. The merger of a Catholic hospital with two nonsectarian hospitals in Kingston, New York, produced demonstrations and a potential antitrust lawsuit that killed the plan. A new organization, Merger Watch, has stopped proposed mergers in Miami, Baltimore, and other cities.

Another counterattack by the religious right has been the passage of restrictive laws in states where conservatives dominate the legislatures. These laws range from the imposition of waiting periods to restrictions on abortion for minors. The approval of one or both parents is often mandated, ignoring the reality that parents may be divorced or separated, and that minors may be unable to communicate with them on abortion.

Although most restrictive laws have been declared unconstitutional in federal or state court, they have become a huge drain on the personnel and finances of the movement. And they fail to grapple with the dominant problem: that a high percentage of abortions are sought by unmarried minors who desperately need sex education in schools, which is an anathema to the religious right.

The attacks on abortion rights demonstrate the power that can be wielded by a small minority. The power of fear has turned doctors' offices and homes into veritable fortresses. Doctors are forced to wear bulletproof vests. Their cars are often equipped with bulletproof glass. Their wives and even their children at school are often treated like prisoners.

The power of the religious right ranges from opposing gun control to pushing textbook censorship, but it ultimately concentrates on abortion. The issue involves almost everyone. It is loaded with inflammatory words like *murder*, which resonate strongly in debate.

Undoubtedly, at the start of the twenty-first century, abortion rights is on the defensive. Its primary weapon, as always, must be organizing. The principal groups in the movement—Planned Parenthood particularly, NARAL, NOW, Feminist Majority, National Women's Health Network to name a few—have excelled in this area. Their ability to draw votes has certainly been proved by the dominant support of women for Clinton in 1996 and Gore in 2000.

Movements are obviously made up of individuals who are impassioned and committed. There is a spiritual—almost a religious aspect—to their lives. They are devoting their humanity toward justice for all. They must pass their dedication to their children. The next generation must be reminded constantly of the desperation of women before 1973. They must read the letters from women I received before then and referred to secret doctors. "In the past two months I doubt my sanity," one woman wrote. A New Jersey husband with a twenty-three-year-old wife and four children told me: "My wife begged me to let her kill herself. I just held her tight and cried like a baby."[11]

Chapter 9

SNEAKING INTO HISTORY: HOW VOLUNTARY STERILIZATION BECAME AMERICA'S CHOICE

When Arthur Schlesinger, Jr. concluded, "Ideas are the great educators," he was paying little attention to those special ideas that sneak into history almost surreptitiously. Voluntary sterilization is a noteworthy case in point. In the short span of forty years, with almost no controversy or fanfare and little mass organizing, it has become the number one method of family planning in the United States.

By the time the birth control pill was released nationally in 1960 and became an overnight success, sterilization was virtually unknown to the public and still tainted by previous associations. The medical profession ignored it. Those few hospitals accepting applications from husbands or wives demanded a lengthy and obnoxious committee process for approval. In almost three years of interviews with Margaret Sanger, I can never remember her mentioning the word. As late as 1971, only a limited number of Planned Parenthood clinics accepted cases.

Yet, today, voluntary sterilization is the most favored contraceptive method in the United States. Thirty-nine percent of couples currently using contraception have chosen female sterilization (27.5 percent) or male vasectomy (11.7 percent). Worldwide, at least 223 million couples have chosen the procedure.

Voluntary sterilization represents the rare example of how a revolutionary idea can be supplemented and enforced by a secondary advantage. Birth control is more restricting; it requires the insertion of a diaphragm or remembering to take the proper dosage of daily pills. Sterilization, however, is permanent and eliminates the constant necessity of thinking of protection. Through minor surgery, it guarantees that the daily problems of memory and inconvenience are no longer applicable.

Still, the historical process of bringing an idea to success requires a drastic change in popular thinking. Men and women had to decide they had borne all the children they wanted (or often no children) and were ready to move on to a completely different stage of contraception. Since sterilizations are medically difficult to reverse, people had to be unshakably certain they wanted permanent protection.

Before historical forces could accelerate the progress of this revolutionary idea, long-range obstacles had to be surmounted. The word *sterilization* itself had dismal connotations. It had originally been used against criminals and social deviants by pressure groups that wanted to prevent such malefactors from conceiving children. Eugenic extremists wanted the insane and feebleminded (even victims of epilepsy) sterilized to purify the race. Starting with Indiana in 1907, this obsession was encoded into state law. By 1970, Virginia had forced sterilization on more than seven thousand people.

In 1927, the U.S. Supreme Court approved a state's right of forcible sterilization in *Buck v. Bell*, which revolved around a hillbilly clan supposedly producing generations of mentally disabled. In a decision written by Justice Oliver Wendell Holmes, noted as the most liberal of the nine justices, Holmes sanctified surgical eugenics by pronouncing that "three generations of imbeciles are enough."[1]

In 1933, the laws of Nazi Germany demanded sterilization. In his crazed pursuit of a pure Aryan race, Hitler ordered the sterilization of thousands of supposedly physically or mentally impaired people whose deficiencies failed to meet Nazi standards.

The Vatican condemned sterilization. In his encyclical *Casti Conubii* in 1930, Pope Pius XI ruled that individuals "are not free to destroy or mutilate their members, or any other way render themselves unfit for their natural functions..." Conveniently, the Vatican overlooked its own previous approval of the removal of testicles from boys in the Sistine Choir so that their voices would not change to a normal, masculine pitch. Many Catholic hospitals ignored the prohibition against sterilization until the Vatican enforced it universally in 1985.

The medical profession had long made voluntary sterilization a pariah and enshrined fecundity as a sacred principle. Unless a patient had convincing medical grounds to end procreation, most hospitals set up male-dominated medical committees that would not even consider sterilization unless a patient had reached the mid-thirties and had already produced three to five children. It was not until the 1970s that a barrage of lawsuits against restrictive hospitals ended such archaic regulations.

The final obstacle to the idea of sterilization was psychological. It had long been believed that sterilization was a form of castration and would diminish or even eliminate the sexual drive. Four medical studies made shortly after 1974 proved that just the opposite was true. By abolishing the worry that a diaphragm was not in place or that a pill had been forgotten, sterilization actually intensified sexual pleasure. All four studies proved that the rate of intercourse between couples was 35 to 68 percent higher than it had been before sterilization, and that 57 percent of couples after sterilization considered their lives together "more harmonious."

Unlike the birth control campaign which was unified by Margaret Sanger's driving and flamboyant personality, voluntary sterilization never had spectacular leadership nor an organization that approached the size of Planned Parenthood. Its origins, in fact, were unimpressive, starting with a group in 1943 called Birth Right which soon became the Human Betterment Association. It was not until 1962 that this nucleus developed the confidence to make its name an explicit description of its purpose, the Association for Voluntary Sterilization.

Again, in contrast to the fiery radicalism of birth control, the pioneers of voluntary sterilization came from the monied or professional classes. Ann Howat and Dr. Helen Edey, a psychiatrist, were wealthy women. Dr. Joseph Fletcher was a professor at Episcopal Theological School in Cambridge, Massachusetts. Dr. Curtis Wood gave up his private practice to make incessant road trips, giving lectures, speaking on the radio, and appearing on TV.

The crucial salesman was Hugh Moore, who had made a fortune founding the Dixie Cup Company and used his money to recruit a professional staff and enlist notables like Arthur Godfrey, who touted the merits of his own vasectomy on his TV show. When a Michigan woman staged a vasectomy party to celebrate her husband's surgery, Moore promoted similar parties across the country. The gala event took place in Bangkok on December 5, 1987, to honor the King of Thailand's birthday. At the King's urging, 1,200 men lined up in a large auditorium, divided into eight treatment rooms, where twenty-eight physicians performed vasectomies all day.[2]

The strategy of the Association for Voluntary Sterilization was education rather than the tumultuous confrontations that characterized birth control and abortion rights. Its posture was almost discreet. It never built a network of chapters, but concentrated on getting its impressive, medical studies to the public through the media and drawing new converts through the testimonials of previous converts.

Still, the campaign that lifted sterilization from maligned word to a prized form of permanent contraception was constantly abetted by the historical forces of the 1960s. When the U.S. Supreme Court's *Griswold* decision of 1965 ruled that the "privacies of life" now had constitutional sanction, the Court overturned not just the last anti–birth control laws but also those state laws that had previously made sterilization a eugenic punishment rather than a method of permanent contraception. The ruling had a triple impact—on sterilization, birth control, and abortion.

The rise of the women's movement added to the historical forces behind sterilization. Feminists stressed that men must carry equal responsibility for family limitation. As more women built careers, the women's movement recognized the advantages of sterilization, and the ensuing demand pressured the medical profession to improve its techniques. Advanced technology as always was critical in carrying an idea to ultimate success.

Female sterilization (cutting the Fallopian tubes) had been developed in England around 1823 and was complex enough to require general anesthesia and a few days hospital stay. Now the development of the laparoscope revolutionized the technique, and made it a relatively simple procedure that could be done in thirty or forty-five minutes under local anesthesia at an outpatient clinic with the patient going home in a few hours.

The laparoscope, a long, thin instrument inserted into the body just below the navel, allowed the doctor to see the tubes and cut or block them either by tying them or using bands, clips, or the application of an electric current. A newer version, called mini-lap, involved an even smaller cut just above the pubic hair, allowing a doctor the same access to the tubes. Essure, another method, requires insertion of a narrow cathetar that blocks the flow of eggs.[3]

Female sterilization affects neither the sexual desire nor menstruation. The chances of pregnancy are less than 1 percent. The risks of internal bleeding or infection are small. Although the cost for a woman runs about twice that for vasectomy, most health insurance and Medicaid cover the procedure.

Male vasectomy, developed in the United States in 1880, had previously been the method of choice because of its simplicity and moderate cost. Performed in a doctor's office or outpatient clinic under local anesthesia, it involves only two small cuts in the skin of the scrotum through which the doctor lifts out two sperm carrying tubes, severs them, and ties or seals the ends. The procedure takes half an hour and requires a day's rest.

Again, the rising demand has produced advanced technology. With the new "no scalpel" surgery, the doctor simply pierces the skin with an instrument and stretches the opening so that tubes can be reached and blocked. No stitches are required. Procedure time has been reduced by half. After tests determine that all sperm have been removed from the ejaculate, the chances of pregnancy with both old and new methods are less than 1 percent. Sperm cells simply die and are absorbed into the body. A study of 10,000 vasectomies by the National Institutes of Health proved a complete absence of medical problems. Sterilized men were no more likely than others to develop heart disease, cancer, or other major illnesses.

An important aspect of the startling increase in sterilization is the demand from single men and women. Doctors often refer such cases to social workers for in-depth counseling to be certain their decisions are firm, but Dr. Robert B. Benjamin in the *St. Louis Park Medical Center Bulletin* points out, "It would appear, in view of the present sexual revolution, that there will be an increasing number of single men requesting sterilization." One case of Dr. Benjamin's was an insurance executive who had impregnated four women and arranged abortions for two of them. Although he enjoyed his work with children in a Big Brother organization, he decided to have none of his own. Dr. Benjamin concludes that sterilization for single men "could help them find more meaning and happiness in life and at the same time protect society by prevention of unwanted pregnancies."

The requests for surgical reversal of a sterilization are rare, at most 2 percent of all cases. Yet, no matter how convinced a man or woman is at the time, there may be later factors that could change their minds. Divorce and remarriage as well as the death of one partner are obvious factors that could lead to a person's decision to have another child in the future. The difficulty of reversals, consequently, must always be stressed.

Reversals for women are more complicated. Sterilization methods that involve the use of plugs or Fallope rings are easier to reverse than chemical techniques, which usually destroy the tissue. With a vasectomy, the method used and the time gap since the procedure affect the chances of reversal. If a large portion of the tube was removed, reversal becomes more difficult compared with removal of only a small part.

Reversal studies for women are still inconclusive, but male success depends on attaining a high sperm count—as high as 91 percent—if reversals are done within ten years, but only 35 percent if more than ten years have passed. The achievement of a pregnancy after reversal runs from 30 to 60 percent.

Remarkably, the demand for sterilization, which began to soar in the 1970s, has been greatest among women in the South. This may possibly stem from an aversion to abortion in fundamentalist areas. The percentage of sterilized Protestants, Catholics, Jews, Hindus, and Moslems runs about the same as their proportion in the general population. Significantly, black and Hispanic women are more likely than white women to opt for sterilization, which may result from the need in lower income brackets to limit families in order to keep a paying job. The "machismo" factor, by contrast, has decreased the demand among black and Hispanic males, who consider an abundance of children proof of their virility.

The high rate among ethnic minorities caused considerable controversy in the 1970s. Radical feminists often claimed that women with little schooling and understanding little English had sterilization forced on them by white doctors determined to hold down the size of minority groups. Certainly, a few cases of such racist medicine were identified. But after the first flurry of accusations, no consistent evidence was revealed. A determined effort by medical groups and the Association for Voluntary Surgical Contraception or AVSC (name changed from Association for Voluntary Sterilization) has put an end to the problem.

Remarkably, the sterilization concept has advanced through each stage to success not only with little public controversy, but with the blessings of Congress. Of its 1997 budget of $22,243,362, $18,598,248 comes from the government's Agency for International Development. The movement has always stressed that sterilization is a medical technique that eliminates the possibility of sperm meeting the egg. This decisive difference from abortion or even the morning-after pill has undoubtedly influenced Congress, along with the fact that one out of ten men have been sterilized and many Congressmen may be included in that group. Congress well knows that rampant overpopulation often leads to economic disaster. Thus sterilization programs in Asia and Africa can help to alleviate inflation and unemployment.

In fact, AVSC (renamed EngenderHealth) has increasingly shifted its emphasis from domestic to overseas operations. It has offices in more than forty countries; most of its staff works abroad. In such countries as Bangladesh, Egypt, and Ethiopia, it has expanded from sterilization programs to reproductive health services in general. Its doctors and nurses supply all types of contraceptives and train local staffs in Russia and the former republics of the Soviet Union, where women had always been forced to depend on abortion, while other reproductive technology was labeled a "dark forest."

Revolutionary ideas obviously have no boundaries. Voluntary sterilization is a superb example of an idea that is applicable to almost every culture and meets the needs of most governments. While birth control requires conscientious use and, in the case of diaphragms, must be properly fitted and inserted (all obstacles when education is scanty), voluntary sterilization depends on just one act, one decision. Its enormous advantage in underdeveloped nations is its permanence.

It could be argued that promoting sterilization overseas carries too many risks for American organizations. Yet, sterilization has a universality that sets it apart. It fits the blueprint for biological evolution. Its usage is expanding constantly. Of all U.S. exports, it is undoubtedly one of the best.

Chapter 10

THE ORIGIN OF IDEAS: BETTY FRIEDAN AND LAWRENCE LADER

Among members of my generation, there was no concept of feminism. We knew, of course, about the rebels who met at Seneca Falls, New York, in 1848 and eventually produced the vote for women through the Nineteenth Amendment to the Constitution. By contrast, Alice Paul's campaign for an Equal Rights Amendment, guaranteeing female equality, had fallen apart by the time I entered Harvard in 1937. At that point, except for a few categories like secretaries, teachers, and phone operators, women were still mainly homemakers until the demands of war production in 1941 swept them into factory assembly lines to replace millions of men in the military.

I first became aware of the possibility of a "new woman" when a Vassar senior I dated, and soon married, inducted me into the radicalism of her college circle. Her maiden name as well as mine appeared on our apartment bell and post box. We kept separate bank accounts. She used her maiden name at her job in radio, and after I enlisted in the Army shortly after Pearl Harbor, she worked at the government's Office of War Information for the next four years. It was established between us that her personhood was independent, and she was guaranteed all social and legal rights.

By a strange coincidence, Betty Friedan, who was a year behind us at Smith College, met a few members of the Vassar radical circle and lived with them in 1942. It was the start of our friendship. And although she has never mentioned that this taste of the new woman helped formulate her ideas, I am convinced that the period stayed deep in her subconscious as it did in mine.

Politics were a critical part of my conversion to the importance of ideas. Although I had been moving to the left and reading Marx in my last years at college, I did not vote for Norman Thomas, the Socialist candidate for president in 1940, but considered the New Deal so integral to the country's survival that I became head of the Harvard for Roosevelt committee.

After the war, I decided that the politician closest to my stand was U.S. Representative Vito Marcantonio, who was Fiorello La Guardia's protégé. He was elected from the East Side of Manhattan from the Sixties to Harlem. This brilliant, rambunctious Italian-American drew huge crowds at street corner speeches and was noted for his limitless attention to his constituents. For years, he had been reelected not just as a Republican, but eventually on the Democratic and American Labor party lines as well. But when the cold war flared up, he was vilified as a Communist as a result of his frequent votes that followed the Communist Party platform. Still, he always wore a Catholic cross, attended church, and could best be described, in my view, as a Christian Socialist.

I soon became one of Marcantonio's district leaders and his public relations consultant. I spent exhausting evenings climbing tenement stairs and soliciting votes for him. When all other parties combined behind one candidate in a highly publicized drive to defeat Marcantonio in 1950, I spent nearly every evening canvassing and speaking on sound trucks in the ten or so square blocks that were my responsibility.

His defeat by a slim margin was a horrific blow to my five-year commitment, and it shook up my previous concept about the importance of political involvement. I decided that electing one, or even a bloc of members to Congress, rarely had much effect on the social direction of the country. In a step that I suppose can be called an epiphany in my life, I concluded that producing a powerful idea and building a movement behind it was the direction that would now dominate my career. I did not know it then—I didn't even start my Margaret Sanger biography until 1952—but convincing the public of the need for family planning and abortion rights would become my passion.

Friedan, too, was being pushed toward her critical ideas of feminism through politics, in her case, union politics. For more than two years after 1943, she worked for the Federated Press, which supplied articles to hundreds of union newspapers. By the end of the war, women made up 36 percent of the labor force, but they were ousted by men discharged from the military. Although Friedan struggled to hold her job, she was finally fired. Her case taught her a bitter lesson about the fragility of women's chances for secure employment.

She was then hired by the United Electrical Workers newspaper. United Electrical (UE) was one of the most powerful unions in the Congress of Industrial Organizations (CIO), and a hefty proportion of its executives and local chapter officials were Communist or under Communist influence. In her brief flirtation with the left, Friedan marched on the San Francisco picket lines of Harry Brydges' longshoremen, another Communist-dominated union, attended Communist front meetings, and even applied (but was turned down) for membership at Communist Party headquarters in New York City.

The UE (proud to retain most female members) assigned Friedan frequent articles on women. Researching and writing these articles increased her awareness about the plight of women. Her most influential writing was a thirty-nine-page pamphlet in 1952 titled "The UE Fights for Women Workers." It analyzed female exploitation, particularly a wage scale lower than men's, and lauded UE's efforts to achieve parity in pay and access to skilled jobs denied women elsewhere. Such research produced ideas that would eventually lead to *The Feminine Mystique*. Yet, Friedan has always blotted out her radical past. Until recently, she never even mentioned her employment at the UE. Like me, she also canvassed on street corners for Marcantonio in 1948 and for Henry Wallace, the Progressive candidate for president. Both of us became frustrated with the shaky gains of electoral politics. Both of us turned to the idea of feminism as a better means for changing society.

Remarkably, our development kept following parallel tracks. After writing articles for *The New Yorker* and *Esquire* in 1945, I started a fifty-year career as a magazine and book writer and occasionally as an editor. Friedan married, moved to Rockland County near Manhattan, and bore three children. She became a magazine writer in 1952. Writing enabled her to work at her house, an advantage as a working mother, and make trips to the city for research. Her frustration with politics was followed by even more acute distress with the role of suburban homemaker. Her articles reflected her present role: she wrote about suburban women organizing day care for *Parents* magazine and an article titled "I Went Back to Work" for *Charm* magazine. Although her subject matter was often superficial, it further grounded her in the problems of working women, which would push her toward her climactic stand on feminism.

We saw each other frequently in this period. She worked, as I did, at the Frederick Lewis Allen writer's room at the New York Public Library, and she joined the Society of Magazine Writers of which I was president in 1958. Although *The Feminine Mystique* was still hidden in her subconscious, we often talked about the emergence of the new woman, particularly after I started my biography of Margaret Sanger in 1952.

In 1957, Friedan prepared a questionnaire for the fifteenth reunion of her Smith classmates. Her classmates' responses became the catalyst for Friedan's move to feminism. Here in vivid detail was all the despair in their lives, the endless cleaning and dishwashing that made them slaves of their husbands, the failure to achieve any satisfactory careers of their own despite a superb Smith education. Friedan grasped the emergence of a social condition that not only enveloped her Smith classmates, but a larger audience as well, which she addressed in an article for *Good Housekeeping* titled "The Problem That Has No Name." Hundreds of letters from readers confirmed her instincts that women were ready to revolt. In a logical advance in her own transition from housewife to combative figure that would mold the direction of her era, she prepared a book outline and W.W. Norton signed her to a contract with a modest advance.

The book, which would become *The Feminine Mystique,* had many gaps. It virtually ignored African-Americans and working women. It only made slight reference to the need for birth control, although I talked to Friedan about Sanger often as we worked together in the Allen Room. She would explain to me later that she was so concentrated on jobs and pay she had not yet understood the crucial link between a woman's liberation and the number of children she bore. Reshaping her own life in *Mystique,* she eliminated her radical past and portrayed herself as a typical suburban mother, which became the audience of her message. The book was a success, and Friedan would stake out the territory of this new wave of feminism on her own.

My own progress from a magazine and book writer to the tumult of being the first male spokesperson for abortion rights was more direct. After seven years of writing for magazines, I decided to do a book. Since I was skilled at profiles, it was logical to take on a biography. The seeds of early feminism implanted by the Vassar group obviously influenced my choice. When I came upon the name of Margaret Sanger in my search and rejoiced at the fire and commitment of her career, I knew immediately I would tackle her biography.

Sanger poured out her most intimate thoughts to me in three years of interviewing, and she would become the greatest influence in my life. She convinced me that women must have total control of procreation to achieve the education and jobs they wanted and a stable relationship with men. But there was a disturbing block in her outlook. She knew almost nothing about abortion since her experience was limited to the hack practitioners who preyed on women during her years around 1912 when she was a nurse in Manhattan. All she could recommend was the chapter of a medical book, which turned out to be dated nonsense.

Meanwhile, I published a study of the New England antislavery movement in 1961, which gave me further insight into the courage of the female abolitionists inspired by the Seneca Falls conference. All this time, abortion haunted me. Medical advances had made it a safe and simple procedure. Yet, when I studied the scientific literature, there were only a few medical papers from Eastern Europe and Japan. The medical profession and the media had imposed a sweeping boycott on the subject for a hundred years.

In trying to fathom how I arrived at the idea of abortion rights in what could be termed a big leap in my thinking, we must examine the social and psychological parameters of my progress. The dominant factor was my dedication to women's rights, engendered by the Vassar radicals and honed by my friendship with Sanger and the history of her crusade. I had always liked the challenge of new adventures, exemplified by the radio station I founded at Harvard, which broadcast programs that dared the status quo. Coming from a somewhat staid family, whom I had previously shocked with my work for Marcantonio, I gladly assumed the mantle of rebellion. I may well have prized the heroic status that abortion rights might give me. I also reasoned that the Montgomery bus boycott and Martin Luther King had produced an ambience favorable for new social pioneering.

The hurdles, however, were severe. I still had to make my living as a magazine writer and worried that the controversy over abortion would damage my relationship with editors. The philosophic hurdles were even more complex, made easier by the Supreme Court's *Griswold* decision of 1965. Its sweeping language on the privacy rights of women I predicted could be applied to abortion as well as birth control.

Still, I had to wrestle with my own personal definition of how religion, medicine, the state, and the individual woman were interrelated. I was completely alone in solving these conflicts; no one had dealt with them before. In years of indecision and debate, my wife became my principal guide. If she ever faced the possibility of abortion, we decided that neither doctor, clergy, nor legislature should interfere with her freedom of choice. Drawing largely on Sanger's concept of inviolable personhood, I would announce that a woman's body belonged to herself alone. Until the moment a fetus emerged from the womb, a woman controlled the fetus she was nurturing.

No single factor, but a blend of the knowledge and instincts of previous decades, had brought me to this revolutionary idea. I drew up an outline for a book, and Bobbs-Merrill, the publisher, accepted it in 1962. Nothing would ever be the same for me and my family again.

Taking the ideas that Friedan and I formulated and building them into a movement required a major leap, however. Friedan has claimed that she did not set out consciously to start a revolution. This is not completely accurate. At the time she agreed to write a plug for my book jacket in 1965, we were discussing how to turn ideas into organizing. The founding of the National Organization for Women (NOW) in 1966 was pivotal. When women leaders like Catherine East from the U.S. Department of Labor and Dorothy Haenen of the United Auto Workers met in Friedan's hotel room, this idea made a big advance toward reality. Friedan's volcanic enthusiasm, bolstered by years of lecturing to women on *Mystique*, made her the obvious candidate for president. Kathryn P. Clarenbach of Wisconsin, chair of the governor's commission on the status of women, was voted chair of the board. At the end of its first year, NOW had 1,200 members.

My first concern in abortion rights was not organizing; it was how to bring an idea to the public in the simplest and most persuasive terms. The *New York Times Magazine* and *Reader's Digest* speeded up this process by carrying my articles on abortion in April 1965 and

May 1966 respectively. When I was deluged with phone calls and letters from women asking for help on abortion, I realized we had reached the stage of confrontation.

After locating skilled doctors around the country who would perform the procedure secretly, I referred at least two thousand women before legalization. I was provoking district attorneys to arrest me and have the courts define the law. This involved blatant risks, of course. I was frequently interrogated by detectives and was summoned to the Bronx Grand Jury. Fortunately, I was never indicted. Our objective, which spurred me and a few pioneers already speaking around the country, was to establish local chapters, which became the National Association for Repeal of Abortion Laws (NARAL).

Although misleading accounts of the convention have been published, the militant faction emphasized that women's rights should become the core of our platform, as I had insisted in my book. We had done a careful job in lining up prominent delegates for complete repeal of punitive laws, approved easily in the final vote. This core idea of women's rights would rule the movement in succeeding years.

Friedan's climactic idea was to organize a Women's March down New York's Fifth Avenue on August 26, 1970, the fiftieth anniversary of female suffrage. She was convinced that previous actions—women demanding service in the all-male Oak Room of the Plaza Hotel, for example—were only peripheral. Women had to show that the movement had become a significant force in American life.

Although there had been small marches before such as at New York's Lenox Hill Hospital or at the state legislature building in Albany, Friedan was determined to draw 10,000 people. Her ideas and strategy were often grounded in her psychological and emotional needs and demands. Her explosive personality and habit of irritating her associates led to her not being reelected NOW president. She wanted an inspiring project to crown her career.

"I had to organize this action on my own," Friedan recalled. By 5 P.M., thousands had gathered at the starting point at Sheridan Plaza. Thousands more joined the march as it swept down Fifth Avenue to 42nd Street. The numbers swelled to at least 20,000, and although the police had only given a permit to march down half the avenue, Friedan took one of her characteristic risks and ordered women to take over the whole avenue.

Friedan had not been able to recruit any congresswomen or other notables to march with her and share the risk at this early stage of the movement. In the frontline, flanked by Friedan and myself, was Dorothy Kenyon, an aged, former municipal court judge who had been one of the few officials to speak up early for abortion rights. The women's march was an impressive example of how ideas could be turned into reality. It was the "high point of my political life," Friedan concluded.

Chapter 11

AN IDEA THAT FAILED: THE EQUAL RIGHTS AMENDMENT

In our examination so far of ideas that revolutionized society, we have not taken account of ideas that failed. Yet, many of them, critical as they may have seemed at one time, created immediate turbulence and then disappeared. The most noteworthy was the Equal Rights Amendment (ERA), which virtually depleted the energies of the women's movement and drained its finances from 1970 to 1982. It could reasonably be described as its greatest disaster, and it needs to be analyzed carefully to prevent such strategic errors from happening again.

The idea of a constitutional amendment, which would guarantee female equality under federal and state laws, was prompted early by enthusiasts as divergent as Eugene Debs, the perennial Socialist candidate for president, and Theodore Roosevelt in his Harvard senior thesis. But an organized campaign was not launched until Alice Paul's National Women's Party in 1923. It sputtered along until 1970, when the women's movement decided to make ERA its focus.

The moment was inauspicious. Abortion rights had been gathering momentum and had reached a decisive stage in 1970 with the passage of the landmark New York state law and similar laws and court decisions elsewhere. The decision of feminists to switch their efforts to the ERA, when the Supreme Court was already considering *Roe v. Wade* and a monumental counterattack against abortion rights was already in the offing, was ill advised.

The first rule in launching an idea, as we have seen, is that it must be rooted deep in the aspirations of society and answer the immediate needs of an individual. Abortion rights fit this formula exactly. It went to the core of a woman's being. Women desperately needed help that would meet not just a momentary but a lasting crisis.

By comparison, the ERA in the 1970s was an imprecise concept. It dealt with such a broad spectrum of political and social issues that the average woman had no feeling of overwhelming urgency and could not grasp how its passage would change her life at the present.

The groups extolling the ERA tried hard to show its impact, explaining that expected protection under the Fourteenth Amendment's "equal protection" clause of the Constitution hardly guaranteed equal property rights to married women and did not even cover the right of jury service. Thus, the ERA for many was just a symbol, a part of feminist ideology; it never acquired the fervor of immediacy.

At the end of years of ERA campaigning, a *Parade* magazine poll showed that on a list of feminine priorities, the ERA ranked only sixth. The first priority was equal pay for equal work. Since women were most concerned about pay and achieving higher positions long reserved for men (breaking the "glass ceiling"), the problem was convincing women that the ERA would fulfill their demands.[1]

The situation was far from clear-cut. Congress had partly answered many demands with the Equal Pay Act of 1963 (although it was still rarely applied). A greater advance was Title VII of the Civil Rights bill of 1964, which banned any discrimination stemming from sex, race color, religion, or national origin. It further guaranteed women equality with men not just in compensation, terms, conditions of employment but in pensions and retirement plans as well. The Pregnancy Discrimination Act of 1978 brought improved conditions for maternal leave. After sixteen states incorporated the principles of the ERA in their constitutions, many women expected the state to protect them and were dubious about the value of the federal ERA.

A constant obstacle was that the ERA campaign lacked a unified strategy. There was a diversity of arguments from different directions. Radical feminists, exemplified by a group called Red Stockings, charged "All men have oppressed women." Another approach was absolutist: Writing in the *Yale Law Journal,* Professor Thomas Emerson stirred up a hornet's nest about women in the military by insisting the ERA should make no compromises and that women must "be eligible for combat duty." Labor unions, too, were split at first. Some worried that the ERA would destroy protections for female workers, such as weight-lifting limitations, already established by legislatures and courts. Although the AFL-CIO eventually backed the ERA, few unions put personnel or money into the campaign.[2]

Another obstacle to the ERA's passage was the lack of experienced and politically skilled leadership. In the tortured route to the New York State abortion law of 1970, the sponsorship of Assemblywoman Constance Cook was indispensable. She was not only a veteran Republican from an upstate rural area and close to Republican Governor Nelson Rockefeller, she was also a tough handler of votes and a convincing debater on the floor while always maintaining an aura of "Mom and apple pie." As chair of NARAL, which organized the state coalition, I was constantly seeking her strategic guidance.

By contrast, only in the last years of the ERA campaign was Eleanor Smeal, as president of NOW, able to achieve anything close to Cook's role. The early ERA coalition was a patchwork. Its so-called Ratification Council had almost no money or staff. Finances eventually improved, and NOW's membership soared to 102,000 by 1982. Still, ERA forces failed to build a strong consensus of voters in swing states like Illinois and rarely competed with the opposition in getting media attention.

Ironically, the ERA campaign suffered at first from overconfidence. The ERA passed the House of Representatives by the resounding margin of 354 to 23 and the Senate by 84 to 8. It had the support of both

Democratic and Republican platforms until the Republicans pulled out in 1980. All presidents except Ronald Reagan and even conservatives, such as U.S. Senator Strom Thurmond, backed it, as did an array of illustrious women including Lady Bird Johnson and Betty Ford.

Then the trouble started. According to the Constitution, two-thirds of the state legislatures had to ratify an amendment after congressional passage. By 1977, the ERA was still three states short. Suddenly, ERA forces were confronted with violent opposition from Phyllis Schlafly and her Eagle Forum and right-wing allies such as the John Birch Society.[3]

Born in 1924, a striking if not beautiful woman with blue eyes and a china-white complexion, Schlafly was a fervent Catholic who had run twice for Congress and lost. She had unstinting political ambitions and realized that an anti-ERA campaign might be her path to prominence. In understanding how political configurations can help or hinder the development of an idea, it should be noted that Schlafly would become the vehicle of a fundamentalist-Catholic conservative alliance. By 1979 "born again" Christianity had achieved respectability, and the Reverend Jerry Falwell had propelled himself onto the political stage under the banner of the Moral Majority. His organization was not mentioned in the *New York Times Index* until 1980. Schlafly and her anti-ERA furor provided the glue for a new right-wing bloc that would inject religious morality into politics and would get the financial backing of Jay Van Andel of the Amway Corporation and Clement Stone, the insurance magnate.

Schlafly's main weapon was fear. She hammered at the theme that the ERA was a "total assault on the role of the American woman as wife and mother and on the family as the basic unit of society." She contended that "God intended the husband to be the head of the family." Playing on female frailty a well as male machismo, she stressed a "woman's continuing need for male protection," and insisted that "If you take away a man's responsibility to provide for his wife and children you're taking away everything he has."[4]

Schlafly depended on exaggeration and never hesitated to twist the truth. Homosexuality became an obsession with her. Insisting that the ERA would lead to unisex toilets and marriage certificates for male couples and female couples, she proclaimed that "NOW is for pro-lesbian legislation so that perverts will be given the same rights as husbands and wives." Clay Smathers, an African-American state representative from Texas demanded the "right to segregate my family from these misfits and perverts."[5]

Obviously, Schlafly and her allies were determined to convince unratified state legislatures that ERA was the tool of liberal feminists, even though 450 mainstream organizations, such as the League of Women Voters and the Association of American University Women, eventually backed it. Reviving the tactics of McCarthyism and red-baiting, Schlafly kept branding ERA proponents as Communists or Socialists. Governor George Wallace of Alabama, presidential candidate of the American Party in 1972, described ERA as a "socialist plan to destroy the home, make women slaves of the government and the children wards of the state." They constantly linked ERA to abortion rights, which was an anathema to right-wing Catholics and fundamentalists.[6]

Concentrating on unratified states, such as Illinois, Schlafly shaped her fury in apocalyptic terms. It was a struggle that pitted federal power against state rights and the family, certain to bring "quasi-criminal anarchy in the home, the workplace, and the school." It was a struggle between the emergence of the new woman and the status quo that would bring a "slide to national suicide."[7]

Pivotal to her argument was the possibility of drafting women into the military. ERA confusion on this issue, with some absolutists claiming women must be eligible for combat, gave Schlafly an easy opening. She trumpeted polls that showed only 22 percent of the public approved of drafting women and using them in combat. She enlisted crowds of teenagers to parade at Illinois legislative hearings carrying signs against the draft and organized similar delegations at hearings in Florida and Oklahoma. No other issue was more botched by ERA supporters. It was the ultimate example that if a new idea is to gain a mass base, it must be clear-cut and simple with no possibility of confusion or misinterpretation.[8]

Schlafly's ploys easily outclassed those of ERA forces. When thousands of women delegates met in Houston, Texas, in November 1977 at the climax of International Women's Year, Schlafly staged counter-demonstrations with balloons and banners that mocked the event as "International Witches Year." She had her female allies bring homemade pies and bread to legislative hearings to prove the anti-ERA position was based on home values. In North Carolina, she assembled two thousand women, praying and singing around the capital building.

One of her shrewdest tactics was to enlist the Mormon Church. Mormons infiltrated International Women's Year delegations, grabbing 63 percent of the delegates from Hawaii, for example, although Mormons made up only 3.2 percent of the state population. Mormons were highly organized. "The structure exists where I can make sixteen calls," boasted a Florida leader, "and by the end of the day 2,700 people will know something." N. Eldon Tanner of the Mormon's First Presidency branded "emancipation, independence, and sexual liberation" of women as "Satan's way of destroying women, and the home and the family—the basic unit of society."[9]

ERA forces were slow at developing strategies that could counter Schlafly's political savvy. Possibly the most effective approach was to announce that no women's conventions would be held in states that had not ratified ERA, a sharp blow to local pocketbooks, but this was not instituted until mid-1978. An ERA march, proving the movement's clout, was held in 1979, when 100,000 people demonstrated in Washington, D.C. Civil disobedience, used so effectively by Martin Luther King and anti–Vietnam War radicals, came even later. In June 1982 in Illinois, women chained themselves to railings in front of the State Senate building and had to be hauled away by police. They infiltrated legislative halls and disrupted proceedings. They sat in at governors' offices and wrote their names in blood on the marble floors of capitol buildings. Finally, they were drawing media attention that had mainly gone to Schlafly.

The ERA's complication at the end was that except for Illinois, unratified states were in the South and Southwest, hardly favorable territory. And Illinois had the special drawback that bills had to be passed by a three-fifths vote.

Pro-ERA legislators came mainly from Chicago as opposed to rural downstate. Chicago became contentious territory when Mayor Richard Daley turned against ERA, and Cardinal John Patrick Cody attacked it furiously, bringing other bishops with him.

Many legislators had ties to the insurance industry, which feared that ERA would destroy the advantage of charging higher rates to women, who, among other stigma, were considered poor credit risks. An analysis by NOW showed that women were charged approximately twice as much as men for medical insurance and disability coverage. The Oklahoma Farm Bureau, owner of insurance companies, lobbied friendly legislators and claimed credit for defeating ERA in that state. In Florida, State Senator Dempsey Barron, whose law firm represented sixteen insurance companies, was instrumental in anti-ERA lobbying.[10]

In 1978, the time allotted by Congress for ratification had run out, and the ERA alliance had to go back for an extension vote. It only passed by 233 to 188 in the House and 60 to 36 in the Senate, far closer than the first congressional approval. Despite intensive concentration on Illinois, ERA failed constantly by a slim margin. On June 23, 1983, the Illinois House passed it by 103 to 72, still 4 votes short of the three-fifths requirement. It was the death knell for an exhausting campaign.

The ERA struggle could logically be compared to Margaret Sanger's long-drawn out effort to pass federal legislation on birth control in the 1930s. Both ventures confronted lopsided odds. Neither Sanger nor the feminists behind ERA stood to gain much if they had succeeded, for other approaches were making faster progress. Neither campaign sought expert analysis before they were launched, and neither was managed by political veterans. Once again, we must accept the principle that every idea needs careful study before it becomes a campaign and needs astute handling when it moves to the stage of public debate and legislative approval.

On the affirmative side, both Sanger and ERA produced significant gains for their causes. They roused the public to nationwide understanding of the issues, and they sharply expanded the membership of their organizations. They not only recruited new leadership, but a huge pool of new members. NOW, in fact, became a national powerhouse, and Planned Parenthood started its ascent, eventually creating hundreds of new clinics, and becoming a dominant force in birth control and abortion rights. Much as both campaigns can be criticized, they became minor milestones in the women's movement and provided training and experience that were invaluable in coming years.

There is considerable irony in the fact that many objectives of the ERA in the 1970s have been secured in 2003. Women serve in combat in some branches of the armed forces. Many colleges and medical and law schools accept a higher proportion of women than men. Women are increasingly being appointed chief executive officers of major corporations. Women's salaries in general still lag behind men's, but the gap has been decisively lessened.

Chapter 12

THE IDEA OF VIOLENCE

At certain propitious times in history, ideas seem to flood society and bring revolutionary change. We must find out why some eras are ripe for change, and how these movements link to each other and bolster each other. We must analyze the decades after 1955 when everything seemed to happen at once: the tumultuous demand for civil liberties by African-Americans, the women's movement, political radicalism, all enveloped by the bitter opposition to the Vietnam War that almost tore the country apart.

The Montgomery bus boycott of 1955 may be an arbitrary starting point, but it logically came toward the end of McCarthyism when the ideals of Roosevelt's New Deal were buried by the mania to crush the Soviet Union and Communism. There is an argument that the ideas of the 1930s, such as social security, had long been stifled not just by McCarthyism, but by the crisis of World War II and the concentration on industrial expansion. Civil liberties may have been the pioneering idea of 1955, but like most ideas, its origins emerged long before.

Although black emancipation had supposedly been guaranteed by the Civil War and subsequent constitutional amendments that produced the election of blacks to Congress, the dream was destroyed by the "deal" of 1876. To secure the election of Rutherford B. Hayes to the presidency, the Republican party bought the needed electoral votes by agreeing to withdraw federal troops from the Old Confederacy states. The South, thereupon, invented a new form of slavery through vicious state laws, a Ku Klux Klan that held blacks in terror, and rampant lynchings and beatings. The North was intent on building an empire and neglected its obligations to former slaves.

Strangely, even the most dedicated abolitionists, like William Lloyd Garrison, believed their goals had been accomplished. With exceptions such as the Northern teachers who ran the schools on South Carolina's Sea Islands, the abolitionists ignored the plight of southern blacks.

A prime example is the government's retreat on the use of blacks in the military. Although 175,000 blacks, many in front-line units, fought in the Civil War and gave the Union a decisive advantage over shrinking, Confederate manpower, African-Americans in World War I and World War II were almost completely confined to trucking and supply duties. Only in late 1945 would a handful of blacks be admitted to Officer Candidate School.[1]

Even with the founding of the National Association for the Advancement of Colored People (NAACP) in 1909, spurred by the militant followers of W. E. B. DuBois, there was only token black organizing in the South through the 1930s. Scattered Congressional attempts to ban the poll tax, once a device to block black voting, failed quickly. The new Congress for Industrial Organizations (CIO) hewed to Communist Party policy by trying to integrate southern unions. One of its rare successes was a 10,000 member local of the Food, Tobacco, and Agricultural Workers in North Carolina. Paul Robeson sang to an integrated meeting of the Southern Negro Youth Congress in Alabama in 1942. The Highlander Folk School in North Carolina, a left-leaning think tank, concentrated on training an integrated leadership for social action. But it was not until Henry Wallace's Progressive party campaign of 1948 that a presidential candidate focused national attention on segregation by refusing to speak to nonintegrated meetings.

Two steps provided the framework for a breakthrough. In 1948, President Harry S. Truman abolished racial discrimination in the armed forces. In 1954, the NAACP's legal team under Thurgood Marshall gained an epochal and unanimous decision in the U.S. Supreme Court in *Brown v. Board of Education of Topeka*, which overturned the "separate but equal" doctrine, long the basis of school segregation.

Given the fury that had been building in the black South (forty-five lynchings within eighteen months of the end of World War II, the recent murder of Emmet Till), the emergence of new strategies was predestined. Southern blacks would no longer settle for court decisions and executive orders. They were ready to confront the system with mass action on a revolutionary scale.

Although most NAACP chapters were slow moving, it was no accident that the setting for rebellion became Montgomery, Alabama. E. D. Nixon, the former president of both the Alabama and Montgomery chapters of the NAACP, had started a black registration drive in 1944. The forty-two-year-old Rosa Parks, his trusted friend, had been trained at Highlander Folk School. They had long been searching for an idea that would incite a confrontation. "The movement didn't spring up overnight," Nixon explained.[2]

On December 1, 1955, Rosa Parks refused to move to the back of her bus in accordance with Alabama law. She was arrested, thereby setting off the black boycott of the city's bus lines, which lasted 382 days. The boycott united a community of 50,000 African-Americans. By striking at the core of the southern system, it would enflame more radical revolts in nearby states.

The boycott further swept Martin Luther King, a twenty-six-year-old minister, into politics. A follower of Gandhi, his policy was confrontation, not passive resistance but active, nonviolent resistance. Couching his concepts in the language of hymns and spirituals, King rejected violence even when bombs were thrown at him and preached, "We must meet hate with love." Involving every black down to the smallest child, King's followers defeated the Southern system for the first time. On November 13, 1956, the Supreme Court outlawed seg-regated public transportation.

The critical issue is whether an idea has enough power to succeed on its own or whether inspirational leadership is essential. The Montgomery boycott may well have been won without King; he had many brilliant associates. But King speeded the process. Barely out of divinity school, he would soon rouse young blacks to apply drastic ideas of their own, and without a rigid framework of leadership.

On February 1, 1960, four black students from North Carolina Agricultural and Technical College walked into nearby Greensboro and sat down at the segregated lunch counter of the Woolworth's store. They were refused service and were roughed up by white patrons, but a dozen blacks came back the next day. The bus boycott had evolved into a different type of confrontation—the sit-in. By April, these sit-ins had spread to seventy-eight southern cities and towns, resulting in the arrest of 2,000 students. Within a year, the sit-ins blanketed the South, 50,000 to 70,000 students forming a black wall of resistance.

Youths as young as fourteen and fifteen joined the movement. They were a new breed, brash in their independence from old-line black groups. They were mainly the children of laborers. John Lewis was the only one of ten children of a poor Alabama family to finish high school. Henry Thomas was raised with nine children in a Georgia shack. "Each kid who went said he was willing to give his life," Lewis reported. These young rebels confronted a mob blocking entry of black students into Central High School in Little Rock, Arkansas, forcing President Eisenhower to call up the 101st Airborne Division to guarantee the law.[3]

The idea of confrontation soon expanded. Students formed lines at white movie theaters, were refused a ticket, and got back into line. They sat at municipal libraries and swimming pools. The cry was "fill the jails." The sit-ins were run like a military campaign. Students sent separate squads to ten restaurants at the same time, making the police frantic, as new squads replaced those just arrested. Struggling to keep up with student militancy in Atlanta, King sat in with fifty-one students and was arrested on October 19, 1960.

By the spring of 1961, when lunch counters and restaurants had been integrated in 140 southern cities, John Lewis, James Farmer of the Congress for Racial Equality (CORE), and militants who dubbed the NAACP a "black bourgeois club" developed the more drastic idea of freedom rides. Although the Supreme Court had prohibited the segregation of interstate travel in 1960, bus segregation was still common in the South. Sit-ins led logically to integrated bus travel for CORE and a fiery new group called the Student Non-violent Coordinating Committee (SNCC), which rejected King's moderate approach.

After incendiary bombs were thrown at integrated buses in Anniston, Alabama, in May 1961, nineteen freedom riders at Montgomery were met by a mob of thousands. Riders were smashed to the ground by baseball bats and iron rods. Even John Siegenthaler, an emissary from the U.S. Justice Department, was knocked unconscious. It took twenty minutes for the police to arrive.

The freedom ride idea had the power to go beyond racial and class lines and drew white volunteers, including the Reverend William Sloane Coffin, Jr., the Yale chaplain, and many Protestant and Jewish clergy. At Jackson, Mississippi, so many riders were arrested for integrating the white waiting room, they filled the city and county jails and eventually the state penitentiary. When the U.S. Interstate Commerce Commission began to impose prohibitive fines on the bus companies, the freedom rider idea for all practical purposes forced an end to segregated travel by late 1962.

How do ideas develop in a new direction? When and why does a movement turn to guns? Robert Williams, a 240-pound ex-marine from Monroe, North Carolina, became the proponent of armed force.

He took out a charter from the National Rifle Association and purchased guns legally. When a Klan parade invaded a black area and shot up black homes, Williams fired back. Stressing that violence should be "only defensive," Williams and his guard in 1961 fired at Klan cars whose riders had fired at black homes. An aberrant figure who symbolized growing black nationalism, Williams announced that the fire bomb was the black's "most effective weapon" and that "burn, baby, burn" was the "most notable cry to come out of America since the Boston Tea Party."[4]

When a group faces overwhelming oppression, there comes a point when actions become more militant. Living constantly under the threat of death changed SNCC's attitude. By 1963, many SNCC offices were posting armed guards at night, and workers slept with their guns by their beds. CORE officials admitted that nonviolence was hardly discussed at meetings anymore. Self-defense became an integral part of the radicalization of both groups.

The Deacons for Defense and Justice in Louisiana patrolled twenty-four hours a day, often exchanging gunfire with night-riders. Charles Evers, brother of Medgar Evers, chair of NAACP in Mississippi and recently murdered, concluded that "nonviolence won't work in Mississippi." SNCC workers described themselves as guerrilla fighters. One observer thought that SNCC's Greenwood, Mississippi, office looked "like a front company headquarters during wartime."[5]

King's nonviolent strategy and the violence emerging in SNCC and the ghettos were tested in Birmingham in 1963, the most segregated large city in the nation. Demonstrators led by King penetrated the downtown areas, where they were terrorized by Police Commissioner T. Eugene "Bull" Connor and his snarling police dogs and high pressure fire hoses. A bomb demolished the house front of King's brother. Six more bombs exploded in black areas. With two thousand demonstrators in jail and the city on the brink of chaos, calm was not restored until the Supreme Court ruled the city's segregation laws unconstitutional.

Although factions in SNCC insisted that ghetto blacks were ready for uprisings, the liberal-labor alliance was convinced that black demands could be met within the system through a civil rights bill. Its march on Washington, D.C., on August 28, 1963, was the stage for King's "I have a dream" speech to an audience of 250,000 and became a part of American folklore. John Lewis of SNCC was pressured into speaking although ordered to cut his most provocative line: "We shall fragment the South in a thousand pieces and put them back together again in the image of democracy." Calling it the "Farce on Washington," Malcolm X claimed all it did was to "lull Negroes for a while."[6]

Such reservations seemed justifiable. While state troopers still rode the streets of Birmingham under Confederate flags, a bomb exploded on Sunday, September 15, 1963, in a black Baptist church killing four girls and injuring twenty-one others. Two more black youths were killed before the end of the day. Relations in SNCC between moderates and revolutionaries seemed strained beyond repair.

Despite the assassination of numerous SNCC organizers during the southern registration drives of the early 1960s, 688,000 blacks were added to the registration rolls (44 percent of those eligible). At Selma, Alabama, on March 9, 1965, King led thousands across the Pettus Bridge, including four hundred Protestant, Catholic, and Jewish clergy. They were met by mounted troopers with bullwhips and chains. A Unitarian minister was beaten to death. Shortly afterward, the wife of a Detroit union member, mother of five, and a Episcopalian seminarian was killed.

During the so-called freedom summer of 1964, black ideas permeated the growing white radicalism. Middle-class volunteers, many from the Students for a Democratic Society (SDS), flooded the South. Here is a prime example of the fusion of ideas, for SDS was essentially a campus-oriented organization, the core of the New Left. While old guard blacks clung to President Lyndon Johnson's administration, officials of SDS, such as Greg Calvert, preached that coalition politics would simply "perpetrate the illusion of democracy and freedom."

In a further fusion of ideas, Malcolm X stressed the connection between the Vietnam War, mainly fought by black soldiers, and America's radical imperialism as early as 1964. By late 1965, SNCC opposed black registration for the draft. SNCC members picketed at induction centers, shouting "Hell no, we won't go."

Stokely Carmichael announced that he would go to jail rather than enter the army. He had survived twenty-five jailings, and had given his radical SNCC group in Lowndes County, Alabama, the symbol of the black panther. The idea of nationalism increasingly dominated the black movement. Ideas had spiraled, almost out of control. At Greenwood, Mississippi, in June 1966, the crowd demanded, "What do we want?" Carmichael shouted, "Black power!" The crowd picked up the chant, which extolled the black man as virile, tough, and dangerous. That slogan climaxed the break between moderates and radicals and destroyed the unity of the civil rights era.[7]

The idea of black nationalism reached its ultimate form in Oakland, California, with a new ghetto group headed by Huey Newton that borrowed the Black Panther name. Its credo was to meet force with force. Each Panther carried a loaded, unconcealed gun (legal under California law) and patrolled the community, inviting confrontation with the police. Panthers established guerrilla warfare in the ghettos. Within three years, they claimed chapters in thirty cities.

The ghettos quickly erupted. In Watts, a section of Los Angeles, rioters hurling rocks shouted, "This is for Selma. This is for Birmingham." The link between northern and southern revolts was established. A torrent of riots in 1967—Cleveland, Newark, Detroit, among others—enlarged the idea of violence. In Detroit, blacks used automatic weapons and tracer bullets to fire on police from rooftops. James Forman of SNCC called it a "revolution where we are part of the vanguard process that seizes and holds power."[8]

The black movement spawned the emerging, white New Left. The SDS, founded in 1960, had no creative ideas of its own at first; its main function was to support the black revolt. It was still groping for a purpose of its own.

The escalation of the Vietnam War finally gave the New Left the strategy of centering its struggles on campuses. In August 1964, President Johnson used the Tonkin Gulf incident to prompt Congress to make a resolution that approved the war without an official congressional declaration of war. For the first time in the fall of 1964, students at the University of California at Berkeley would make the campus their battleground. Their clarion call was that the university was no longer an educational institution but a tool in the Vietnam War, "a factory that turns out certain products needed by industry and government."

The uprising started with the administration's ban on SNCC and CORE setting up tables outside a university gate, where they raised money. After student arrests, a police car was held hostage by demonstrators for 30 hours, and the university summoned 643 police officers and state units to disperse the crowd. When 1,500 students took over the administration building, the police dragged them out—"their boots landing heavily on heads, arms, shoulders and legs," a reporter noted. Almost 600 were convicted of trespassing and jailed. Students called a general strike. After the Academic Senate voted overwhelmingly in support of student demands, the uprising was over.

The New Left had taught the public the connection between Berkeley and the Vietnam War. When Berkeley students later sat on railroad tracks to block black troops headed for the embarkation port, the New Left finally organized a coherent plan.

The New Left wanted to reach a wider audience on Vietnam and began teach-ins on 120 campuses in 1965. Martin Luther King temporized at first, but by 1966, he called for an immediate end of the war and led a peace march to Chicago's city hall. He demanded that "somehow this madness must cease."[9]

The New Left capsulated its ideas in a slogan: "The streets belong to the people." At its Spring Mobilization Against the War in Vietnam on April 15, 1967, almost 500,000 demonstrators marched through New York, San Francisco, and other cities. At Oakland, California, in October, 10,000 surrounded the induction center, threw up barricades, and clashed with the police.

As the finale of Stop the Draft Week, the New Left planned an assault on the Pentagon on October 21, 1967. After preliminary speeches at the Lincoln Memorial, a hard core of 75,000 marched on the Pentagon, mainly from SDS and New York's "Revolutionary Contingent," many wearing helmets and fencing jackets. One unit broke through a line of soldiers and surged up a ramp; another unit reached the central plaza. A few fought their way into Pentagon corridors. Paratroopers from the 82nd Division smashed heads with their gun butts. One thousand four hundred were beaten and gassed, 7,000 arrested.

Violence against the war reached its peak in 1968 and was a factor in forcing President Johnson from the White House. The student uprisings in France, which almost overthrew DeGaulle, influenced the New Left. Ideas are easily transplanted, as the impact of the American Revolution on France demonstrated earlier, but need a social framework, which the unions gave the French students in 1968. Union support was missing, however, in the United States.

The New Left came to the Chicago convention in 1968 essentially to make the Democratic Party accept a peace plank. There were no union forces behind them, and Mayor Richard Daley allowed police brutality to take over the city. Demonstrators were slammed against the side of the Hilton Hotel, beaten savagely, and even pursued into the lobby. All these scenes were carried on national television. The Democratic Party allowed this bloodletting except for a last-minute protest by Eugene McCarthy, the only Democratic peace candidate following Senator Robert Kennedy's assassination a few months before.

The Black Panthers forced a coalition with whites against the Vietnam War. J. Edgar Hoover called them the "greatest threat to the internal security of this country." But what changes did this growing coalition really bring? What power did their ideas (except for the immediate result of dumping Johnson) have in revolutionizing America? Certainly, the black rebellion had the most impact. If the ideas of the Montgomery boycott and student sit-ins had not erupted in 1955 and 1960, they would have come soon after. Young blacks could not be restrained; they only needed techniques for action.[10]

It was no accident that King had come to Memphis to support the economic demands of the garbage workers in 1968 when an assassin gunned him down, setting off another storm of ghetto burnings and armed conflict. It was no accident either, that J. Edgar Hoover had long hounded King and had used every illegal device to destroy him, the Black Panthers, and what he considered Communist cells in the New Left.

In the long run, African-Americans made sizeable gains from the volatile ideas of this era. To cite just a few obvious ones, they have elected high officials in the South (and North as well), even from the ranks of SNCC radicals such as John Lewis. They have been admitted in increasing numbers to the best universities and achieved status and advancement in medicine, law, and other professions.

The failures, however, are equally obvious. Bussing of students has rarely corrected the deficiencies of urban schools. Affirmative action, giving blacks and other minorities greater access to jobs, has been met with growing debate and hostility.

Yet, the pioneering ideas of the 1960s continue to produce notable examples of progress. In Birmingham, a city that once saw Bull Connor's snarling police dogs and the murder of children at Sunday school, a black minister was appointed in 2001 to the pulpit of a predominately white and conservative United Methodist Church.

By contrast, the ideas of the New Left have had minimal influence. Once its strategy was divorced from campus organizing and Weather splinter groups rampaged through Chicago to "bring the war home," Weather groups lost touch with reality. Their symbolic finale was in an elegant Federal townhouse on Manhattan's 11th Street in 1970 when an explosion, probably from a misconnected wire in the assembly of bombs, demolished the building. Three bodies were found in the rubble; at least three members of the Weather cell escaped.

As President Richard Nixon opened a new front in Cambodia, the *Black Panther* newspaper listed 423 attacks on police stations and 101 on military installations in 1970. The shooting down of four students at Kent State University by the Ohio National Guard that May marked the last gasp of protest.

Students have remained surprisingly aloof in recent decades from issues of social and political consequence with occasional exceptions such as student demonstrations at Harvard University against the low wages paid the university's menial employees. Yet, there are signs of resurgence. At meetings of the World Trade Organization (WTO), thousands of protesters have battled the police (with numerous injuries) in their anger that the WTO has aided the rich rather than the poor. The Earth Liberation Front (ELF) has launched a series of burnings of buildings to protest timber-cutting projects that it claims are destroying forests and natural preserves. ELF insists that it has threatened no human life. The FBI so far has been unable to stop it or penetrate the cells.

While the ideas of the black rebellion and the New Left have constantly interconnected and amplified each other, the women's movement has developed on its own. Radical, black women at first held little more than servant roles. Panthers clung to the thesis that birth control and abortion were white, racist plots to diminish the black population until women convinced the leadership to accept a woman's right to limit her childbearing. By 1976, when Huey Newton fled the country, two women were elected to the Panthers' top positions.

Stokely Carmichael reputedly announced that the "only position for women in SNCC is prone,'" and the New Left glorified this attitude. Women were mainly coffee-getters and typists. The SDS uprising at Columbia University in 1968 was "completely sexist" according to participants. At an antiwar rally in 1969, men in the audience interrupted a feminist with shouts of "Take her off the stage and fuck her." Robin Morgan concluded in an article: "Goodbye to the Weather-Vain, with its Stanley Kowalski image and theory of free sexuality but practice of sex on demand for males." Women had only 6 percent of SDS executive committee seats in 1964. No woman held national office until 1966, and then only assistant national secretary.[11]

After the founding of the National Organization for Women in 1966, New Left feminists increasingly realized that revolutionary ideas were far more attainable through their own organizations. The New Left was splintering into chaos. The women's movement had the potential to become a dominant, national force. "We had arrived at the point where women's issues had to come before leftist issues," insisted Susan Brownmiller author of *Against Our Will*. Shulamith Firestone in her book *The Dialectic of Sex* saw "feminist issues not only as women's first priority, but as central to any larger revolutionary analysis."[12]

With the rise of the women's movement, the era of violence was over. It is essential to ask: What is the sanction for violence? What can it accomplish? Violence often depends on our perspective. When used by white Americans in an expanding, westward empire that swallowed up the lands of native Americans and Hispanic peoples, it was considered acceptable. The violence of black rebels and the New Left has always been considered criminal.

We must thus define two historical traditions: sheer terrorism in contrast to constructive violence. In the first category, the Baader-Meinhof group in Germany in the 1970s existed in a vacuum of purposeless bloodshed. Although the New Left claimed that only violence could stop the Vietnam war, its bloodshed eventually became pointless and the politics of despair.

Moral justification and historical necessity are basic if we are to condone constructive violence. Black violence in the South after 1955 was an obvious necessity to overcome almost a century of illegal lynchings and terror. Violence by Israelis in ousting the British from Palestine was supported by two thousand years of yearning to reclaim their homeland, the legal imprimatur of the Balfour Declaration, and the urgency of a sanctuary for survivors of the Holocaust.

But what of abolitionists before the Civil War? When they used violence to block the return of fugitive slaves to the South, their justification was the total, moral evil of slavery. Even though they were breaking the law of man, they appealed to the "higher law" of God. John Brown may well have butchered proponents of slavery in Kansas, and he certainly caused needless deaths in his ill-conceived plot at Harper's Ferry. Yet, he was quickly elevated to heroic status by a nation that considered any blow against slavery a historical necessity. The debate hinges on the question of which side has the strongest claim to morality and the higher law of God. No solution may be adequate. It can be asked what good the appeal to "Nature's God" in the Declaration of Independence would have done for rebelling colonists if they had lost the war.

Chapter 13

GUN CONTROL

After an assassin tried to kill President Ronald Reagan in 1981 and seriously wounded his press secretary, Jim Brady, public horror suddenly focused on gun violence. Another accidental event increased general outrage. In 1993, Carolyn McCarthy's husband was murdered on the Long Island Rail Road outside New York City. There had only been haphazard attention to gun control before then. Historical forces may propel a stagnant idea to the center of debate through a planned campaign, as in the case of Charles Bradlaugh's trial in Britain in 1877. Or they may be accidental as with the Brady and McCarthy tragedies which quickly gave an idea public structure.

The increasing slaughter of students across the country by gun-wielding peers intensified this incipient campaign. Gun violence took the lives of 30,708 people in 1998, and an estimated 125,000 people are shot each year. The country was plunged into what a litigant called "one of the titanic political struggles in modern American history."[1]

The struggle immediately became a head-on conflict with the politically powerful and well-financed National Rifle Association (NRA). Claiming, but never proving, a membership of a least three million, it draws on almost a third of U.S. households that owns guns. Its language is volatile, branding the Bureau of Alcohol, Tobacco, and Firearms, the only federal agency delegated to regulate guns, a "group of jack-booted thugs." Its flamboyant front man is the ultraconservative movie star Charlton Heston. Its theoretical base is the Second Amendment to the

U.S. Constitution, which declares: "A well regulated Militia, being necessary to the security of a free State, the right of people to keep and bear arms shall not be infringed."

But what exactly does this amendment mean? Does it mean people can bear arms only as a part of a state or local militia? Or does it give unbridled scope to anyone, criminals included, to own any amount of firearms, even secretly carried handguns?

Despite a U.S. Supreme Court decision in 1939 (*U.S. v. Miller, 307 US 174*) limiting the Second Amendment's purpose to ensuring the "efficiency of a well-regulated militia," the NRA has never budged in its support of the second interpretation that anyone has the right to own any amount of firearms. Although many of its members are sportsmen who make an effort to teach their children how to handle hunting equipment safely, a large proportion of the NRA belongs to an impassioned, conservative fringe that dreads intervention of federal and local governments into their lives. They have no faith in the protection of the law. They treasure their arms as a bulwark against the menace of indefinable, outside intruders.

Randy Weaver of Montana, who was involved in a deadly shootout with federal agents, branded the government a "tool of sinister outside forces." David Trochman of Montana's Alpha Unit, a type of outcast militia, insists his arms protect him against "300 families in the world" that "plan global conquest." Yet, a study shows that guns in the house are twenty-two times more likely to kill someone you know than a potentially dangerous intruder.[2]

Such perverted views among NRA members give the organization an irrational quality that runs counter to the beliefs of most Americans. A *Newsweek* poll in 1999 showed that 74 percent wanted the minimum age for gun possession raised from eighteen to twenty-one years; and a medical association poll revealed 88 percent favored childproofing (such as trigger locks) for handguns. Unfortunately, new legislation has lagged far behind public opinion as a result of the NRA's money and political clout in Congress, particularly through U.S. Representative Tom DeLay, the majority whip and an NRA member.[3]

The NRA's contributions of millions have kept scores in Congress beholden to its platform. Its strength is predominant in the South where gun ownership is high. In the 2000 elections, the NRA spent $25 million in various forms of political contributions and was probably more instrumental in electing George W. Bush than any other group. Bush's attorney general, John Ashcroft, carries an NRA membership card.

Political power stems not only from gun owners but from manufacturers whose profits help to keep legislatures committed to the correct dogma. Approximately two million handguns are sold each year. Sales are international as well as domestic. In 1999, the United States licensed more than $40 million in light weapons for export. The United Nations estimates that more 500 million illegally acquired guns circulate around the world and has tried to limit such trafficking through a pact whose wording President Bush insisted on diluting.

Public momentum behind the idea of gun control was minimal until a startling event, often essential to progress, happened on March 30, 1981. An assassin's bullet, meant for President Reagan, struck Press Secretary Jim Brady over his left eye and passed through the frontal lobe of his brain. Fortunately, it was a small caliber bullet; the brain was not severely damaged. Brady had to undergo more than six hours of surgery. Afterward, his wife, Sarah, gave every moment to his health. His recovery has only been partial and left him generally confined to a wheelchair.

Sarah decided to devote herself to gun control legislation, which soon put her at odds with the Republican Party. Then forty-six years old, she had always been a Republican and had worked for the party for ten years. But as many GOP legislators shredded the aims of what became known as the Brady Bill, she announced, "I am furious at the Republican Party." She founded the Brady Campaign to Prevent Gun Violence.[4]

The momentum behind the idea of gun control was soon augmented by a frightening succession of murders of students by other students. In 1997, three students were killed at a prayer meeting in West Paducah, Kentucky, and a mother and three students were murdered in Pearl, Mississippi. In 1998, three students and a teacher were killed in Jonesboro, Arkansas, and two students were killed in Springfield, Oregon. In 1999, twelve students and a teacher were murdered at Columbine High School in Littleton, Colorado. Between 1994 and 1998, 256 children died from gun shots. Guns have become the leading cause of death for teenage boys in America.

We can find extraordinary proof in the case of Carolyn McCarthy of how an idea depends on the initiative of a few individuals. The murder of her husband not only pushed her to campaign for gun control, it made her take the ultimate step of running for Congress to give the broadest platform to her ideas.

On December 7, 1993, McCarthy's husband, Dennis, and their son, Kevin, were taking a Long Island Rail Road train at 5:33 P.M. from their work in New York City to their home in Mineola. Carolyn McCarthy arrived home to find they had not set up the Christmas tree, still in the driveway. Then her brother told her about a bloody orgy of murder. A passenger had pulled out a 9-millimeter gun (bought in California and transported illegally to New York) and sprayed the car with bullets. Her husband had been killed along with five others. Many, including Kevin, were badly wounded. The killer emptied his gun of fifteen bullets and was overcome by other passengers as he tried to reload.

Kevin, twenty-six years old and their only child, was shot in the head and partially paralyzed. With one-seventh of his brain blown away, he was in a coma for weeks. The doctors gave him a 10 percent chance for survival.

"I fell apart but only for five minutes," McCarthy recalled. She had been trained as a nurse and tended to him during six months of hospitalization and rehabilitation. Although unable to walk or talk for months, Kevin eventually was able to commute to his job in New York, get married, and study at night for his master's degree in business.[5]

The idea of becoming a prominent campaigner for gun control and running for Congress came to McCarthy almost by chance. She had been brought up as a Republican in Republican-dominated Nassau County, living in the same house for forty years. She had always been a housewife except for her nursing and was never involved in politics. But when she decided to do something about gun control, encouraged by her son, she testified for Governor Mario Cuomo of New York on an assault weapons bill.

When Dan Frisa, the Republican member of the House of Representatives from her district and an NRA supporter, voted to repeal the assault weapons ban, she was furious. Her father and two brothers were members of the boilermakers union. Many Long Island unions, upset at Frisa's conservatism on most issues, had been looking for a replacement.

The actual moment of McCarthy's decision had an accidental setting, but months of her mounting anger impelled it. A reporter stopped her on the Capitol steps after Frisa's vote and asked if she was angry enough to run against Frisa for the House. Without thinking, she said she'd consider it seriously. The next day papers all over the country reported that she might be running. The media, in effect, had forced a decision. On May 31, 1996, she announced she was running on the Democratic ticket.

In a disparaging reaction, the chair of the Nassau Republican Party described the new candidate as a "little blonde girl with ponytails." McCarthy retorted she was running because "I want to make sure no family has to go through what we went through."[6]

She may have been a political amateur, but her daring had caught the imagination of the public. She was deluged with phone calls and letters offering money and help. Overnight the power of an idea had overcome the usual campaign obstacles, and the flood of volunteers became a structured, political organization. The decisive factor came when Emily's List (a group giving funds to women candidates) decided to back her financially and assigned an experienced staff member to work with her. Further contributions, mainly $25 and $50, poured in from across the country. Unions contributed. Republican leaders tried to talk her out of running, but many of her Republican volunteers insisted she stay in. "I was in a daze for weeks," she remembered.[7]

Although the basis of her campaign was gun control, she backed most feminine issues, including family planning and abortion rights. As a nurse, she had seen a woman almost die after being forced to have an unwanted pregnancy. McCarthy remained a church-going Catholic, but she considered contraception and abortion personal matters that should not be dictated by the Vatican. She even supported the necessity of late abortions in medical emergencies.

Her campaign built her as the neighbor next door; papers labeled her the "gentle woman from Long Island." She never bashed Republicans and made a personal organization that drew increasingly on Republicans. She was a new and refreshing type of political figure, a highly attractive woman who had wit and charm and could debate issues with both vigor and reasonableness.

All these attributes produced a stunning victory by a 17 percent margin in 1996. But in the next election, her volunteers became over-confident and didn't pull out the vote. She won by only 3 percent. McCarthy made sure that never happened again. In the 2000 and 2002 elections, she took a dominant percentage of the vote and finally made the district her own fiefdom. "She was a very quiet person," her son remarked, "but she turned out to be a leader."[8]

In her first weeks on the House floor, she wore a baseball cap. When the sergeant at arms told her that a baseball cap didn't fit the House dress code, she had to give it up. Her long ponytail now became her signature, as well as the red dresses and sneakers she often wore.

Working late at night, she would often be escorted home by another House member to an apartment house tenanted by others in Congress. Newt Gingrich, sitting on a patio of a nearby restaurant, saw her once and concluded, "You must be dating Mr. X." After that, she decided to walk home alone. Now ten years after her husband's death, she is thinking of having formal dates again.[9]

Carolyn smokes cigarettes but only privately, never at a meeting or before constituents. She is startlingly frank. Once at a smoker following brandy and cigars, she told a prominent justice of the Supreme Court, "You talk and write too much."

Despite incessant campaigning for gun control by Sarah Brady, Carolyn McCarthy, and new organizations devoted to their objectives, little effective legislation has passed. The Federal Crime Act of 1994 banned the future manufacture and sale of some assault weapons. The Brady Bill of 1994 requires state or local law enforcement to conduct background checks on prospective handgun purchasers for felon records (domestic violence added later). However, the three-day period for checking hardly limits criminals who can get their guns through the underground, pawnshops, and exempt private dealers. And the U.S. Supreme Court eroded the bill further by knocking down the mandatory requirement of police checks. Only Maryland and New York require gun makers to provide test-fired samples of bullets when they sell a gun.[9]

State laws have been similarly eroded. Although California and at least sixteen other states have tried to make manufacturers and retailers liable for the costs of gun violence, the California Supreme Court in 2001 overturned the law. Consequently, there is still no law requiring *all* gun purchasers to go through a background check, no law mandating safety locks on all guns, and no law saying all gun sellers and buyers must have a license. Still, California now requires handgun owners to pass a written test, prove they can handle a gun, and supply a thumbprint; and removed the immunity from lawsuits against the gun industry.

Carolyn McCarthy's recent aim has been to control the gun "bazaars." There are at least five thousand of them annually. Almost anyone can buy any gun they want in bazaars that have been called "Tupperware parties for criminals." McCarthy is the sponsor of a bill in the House that would subject these bazaars to all current federal and state restrictions, minimal as they may be at the moment.

McCarthy and Brady were critical movers in the immense outpouring of public indignation against gun violence known as the Million Mom March. When the march was announced on the Internet, march headquarters was getting 75,000 hits a day. The idea galvanized the country. On Mother's Day, May 12, 2000, almost a million people, mainly women, demonstrated in Washington, D.C., and in other cities nationwide.

The idea of gun control seems to have followed all the historical steps to produce success. People were roused by the horror of the Brady and McCarthy shootings, by the frightening succession of student murders, and finally by the Million Mom March. Yet, solutions have been minimal. The record of meaningful legislation has been shockingly poor. What has held back an idea that polls show most of the country favors?

The obvious answer is the political power of the NRA. Through its money and hard-core votes, it dominates the House of Representatives and a nucleus of key senators. The NRA opposes even the slightest legislative change.

Still, other ideas have confronted determined foes and achieved success. Abortion rights, for one, has had to grapple with the Catholic hierarchy and right-wing fundamentalists. It had to convince the country that the availability of abortion was critical to every woman's health and life. Gun control has had a problem in rousing nationwide commitment. In a situation that seems parallel to the campaign for the Equal Rights Amendment, it has not been able to make gun control everyone's dominant concern. Most parents fail to grasp that the next school shooting may involve their child, that the next office assassination may terrorize their workplace.

Abortion rights always depended on local organizing. From 1969 on, when the National Abortion Rights Action League was founded, fiery and disciplined chapters incessantly lobbied federal and state legislators with their platform. Planned Parenthood and the women's movement quickly formed a cohesive political force.

In this essential area of lobbying, gun control has lagged behind. New groups have formed, to be sure. The Million Mom March headquarters and the Brady Campaign to Prevent Gun Violence have merged. And the Soros fund and other foundations are giving supportive grants. Yet, gun control still lacks a national umbrella organization with a huge structure of state and local chapters that can deliver the votes year after year and threaten the legislators: We have produced more votes than the NRA; we have more money than the NRA. Support us or you'll lose the next election.

The Twin Tower disaster of September 11, 2001, has further shown the difficulty of reaching a consensus on gun control. Gun control advocates stress the need to block legal loopholes that allow potential terrorists to buy weapons at gun shows without background checks. One terrorist group member was observed buying weapons at a gun show that were to be smuggled to Lebanon. Another testified in federal court that he had bought weapons at a gun show to smuggle to the Irish Republican Army. Faith Whittlesey, a U.S. delegate to the United Nations Conference on Small Arms, insists that September 11 strengthened the argument that in 1776 "small arms in the hands of private individuals were the means used to secure liberty and independence"[10] U.S. Senator Dianne Feinstein retorted that these were

NRA delegates: "California wants controls on weapons. It has 34 million people—this isn't a peanut of a state."

The irony is that many Democrats, such as Bob Ream, chairman of the Montana Democratic Party, are distancing themselves from the generally antigun stance of the Democratic Party. Women at Mount Holyoke College in Massachusetts have even formed the Second Amendment Sisters and armed themselves with guns. Since September 11, gun sales have soared.

The progress of an idea from origination to success depends on a highly professional and skillfully managed organization that brings constant pressure on legislators. Ideas eventually depend on political dominance. Otherwise, Congress generally brushes aside the pleas of individuals. "How many people have to die before Congress can act?" Carolyn McCarthy demands.[11]

Chapter 14

DEATH WITH DIGNITY:
THE MOST CONTROVERSIAL IDEA

My sister, Helen, was dying of Parkinson's disease in a Florida hospital recently. The doctors announced there was no further useful treatment. Her four children and I agreed that the time had come for a peaceful and dignified death, which could have happened almost instantly with a heavy dose of morphine. But that would have been euthanasia, prohibited under state law. Instead, my sister, who had signed papers years before rejecting artificial feeding and hydration in such an emergency, was forced to die of hunger over thirteen days. Her children had to sit at her bedside watching this barbaric practice while she shrank away to a virtual skeleton and finally stopped breathing.

This is the kind of horror inflicted on thousands of Americans each year who are denied the right to "determine the time and manner of one's death," as Judge Stephen Reinhardt defined it in his majority opinion in the Ninth Circuit of the U.S. Court of Appeals on March 6, 1996. By contrast, the U.S. Supreme Court ruled on June 26, 1997, that "assistance in committing suicide is not a fundamental liberty interest protected by the Due Process clause," and that state laws against assisting a suicide are not unconstitutional. The Court, thereupon, threw the tangle back to the states.[1]

Except for a new law in Oregon, the United States has thus been left in a chaos of conflicting interests. The idea of death with dignity (rarely called euthanasia today because of the word's Nazi taint) has gained momentum, as most people demand that we die on our own terms with our integrity intact. Polls show that 50 to 75 percent of the public support the legalization of medically assisted suicide at the choice of a fatally ill patient.

This momentum behind an idea is partly the result of a historical progression giving individuals control of their destiny, as we have seen in movements like abortion rights. Its immediate impetus, however, stems from the technological advances of medicine. No longer do the elderly die at home from the expected consequences of a heart attack or pneumonia. Today, most patients spend their last months or years in hospitals, kept alive by an astonishing array of transplants, feeding tubes, respirators, and antibiotics.

Medical interests generally dictate that every device be used to keep the patient alive although the patient or family often oppose it. Doctors worry about the possibility of malpractice lawsuits, or that giving a patient a "humane overdose" could result in a loss of license or even prison. State legislators worry about voting for assisted suicide laws against the fury of right-to-life opponents and cite the example of former Governor Richard Lamm of Colorado who was defeated for his controversial views supporting such legislation. We are thus involved in a web of hypocrisies involving medicine, the courts, and politics that is bound to make death with dignity one of the most volatile decisions of this century.

Charlotte Perkins Gilman, the noted feminist stricken with cancer, wrote before her suicide on August 17, 1935, "it is the simplest of human rights to choose a quick and easy death in place of a slow and horrible one."[2]

Elvin O. Sinnard's personal declaration in the case of *Compassion in Dying v. State of Washington* in 1994 describes eleven years of pain suffered by his wife, Sara, that became "unbearable." He stated, "She wanted to die but we didn't know how to do it." Her doctors refused to help. The Sinnards finally chose the method of plastic bag suffocation, but she insisted he leave the house. "I was denied the right to be with her when she died." The police told him "We would recommend indictment if we could establish a direct action on your part in the suicide." "My act was a loving act, not a criminal act," said Sinnard.[3]

In another declaration in 1994 in the Washington State lawsuit, Tania Bloom testified that "my father was dying of lung cancer and was in excruciating pain. His doctor would not prescribe pain medication other than Tylenol saying that to do so 'would not be medically advisable.' When he [my father] realized that my family was going to be away for a day, he wrote a beautiful letter, went down to his basement, and shot himself with his 12-gauge shotgun. This was a brutal and awful experience for my children and me. [A son-in-law had to clean the splattered brains off the wall.] I feel a great deal of loss, anger and remorse about a system that would not allow my father to die gracefully and with dignity."

Summarizing this system, Timothy Quill, M.D., an advocate of reform, concludes: "Current ethical and legal prohibitions reenforce self-deception, secrecy, isolation, and abandonment."[4]

Along with other ideas like birth control that go to the core of human choice, the right to a dignified death originated more than two millennia back. Lucius Annaeus Seneca (c. 4 B.C.–65 A.D.) promoted suicide in his *Epistles* and *De Ira*. "When age once begins to shatter my understanding and impair my faculties. . . . I will leap in haste from the rotten and tottering structure." He insisted, "So I will choose my death when I am about to depart from life."[5]

The Roman Catholic Church denounced suicide and refused burial of the body. Still, Sir Thomas More (1478–1535), canonized by the church, advocated medically assisted suicide as a release from hopeless pain, as did Frances Bacon (1561–1626) in *New Atlantis*. David Hume of Scotland insisted in his essay *On Suicide* in 1776 that "Suicide may be consistent with our duty to ourselves." Thomas Jefferson called it justifiable, particularly in cancer cases. Influenced by Montesquieu, Diderot, and Voltaire, France legalized suicide by a statute of 1790 and repealed all sanctions against the body and property of the suicide.

Here we see the same pattern that characterized the progress of birth control and abortion rights: advanced thinkers staking out philosophic and social grounds. The right to die is rooted in eighteenth century concepts of natural law, which the Founders made basic to the Declaration of Independence.

The first legislation in the United States was introduced into the Ohio House of Representatives in 1906 at the request of Ann Hall, wealthy daughter of an Arctic explorer, and soundly defeated. Similar attempts were made in the Nebraska bicameral legislature in 1937, sponsored by Inez C. Philbrick, M.D., and in the New York legislature in 1938 and following years, backed by 1,776 physicians. A ministers' petition declared: "We believe in the sacredness of *personality* but not in the worth of mere existence of 'length of days.'" Both bills were defeated.[6]

These first advocates of an explosive idea had no groundswell behind them. In England, the idea began to rouse debate in 1932 when Killick Millard, M.D., came out for euthanasia in an address to the Society of Medical Officers of Health. A Voluntary Euthanasia Society was formed under the presidency of Lord Moynihan, president of the Royal College of Surgeons, with such noted members as H. G. Wells and George Bernard Shaw. The first bill in Parliament in 1936 was a failure.

The Euthanasia Society of America followed in 1938, promoted by Dr. Charles Francis Potter of the First Humanist Church. Colonel Robert G. Ingersoll, the radical polemicist and feminist; Simeon E. Baldwin, chief justice of the Connecticut Supreme Court; and Charles Eliot Norton, professor of fine arts at Harvard, all advocated death with dignity.

Yet, the idea gained adherents slowly because of the obstacles against it. The birth control pill prevented ovulation, thereby simulating infertility. The morning-after pill acted before a sperm met the egg, so most of the public was unconcerned about interference with incipient life. The death with dignity campaign, however, dealt with human beings who were generally elderly and often in such poor health that they had trouble coming to grips with the most fundamental decision they would ever make. It not only meant reaching a conclusion with a mate, partner, and family members; it also meant sorting out a complex of medical opinions and weighing the possibility of health gains against the dread of weeks or months of agony. Death with dignity thus confronted a host of conflicting factors, not the least being its impact on society as a whole.

Death has become an imponderable issue today as a mounting number of Americans survive into old age. The elimination of most childhood diseases, the effectiveness of preventive medicine, the rapid advances in medical technology are just part of the reason why the over-sixty-five age group, making up 13 percent of the total population in year 2001, is expected to make up 20 percent or 70 million people by 2030. The over-eighty-five age group is expected to double by 2030.

The elderly, consequently, exert a profound effect on the nation's health care budget as well as the budgets of hospitals and nursing homes. Twenty percent of health dollars are spent on the last two months of life, with the young paying an ever-larger burden of health and Social Security costs. National health care expenditures were $245.8 million in 1980. They rose to $1,311.1 million in the year 2000 and are expected to reach $ 2,637.4 million by 2010.

Increasing longevity has intensified the problems of keeping the elderly at home. Sophisticated medical treatment may be difficult to administer. Apartments are rarely large enough. Even a commodious house may be ruled out by the economic necessity of both wife and husband holding full-time jobs. As a result, more elderly are being forced into nursing homes. The seriously ill are resorting to hospices, an effective and innovative addition to terminal care.

Middle-aged children have a further complication. With their parents living to eighty or more, they will often be in their sixties and plagued with their own infirmities and lower income after retirement. The elderly may openly or subconsciously accuse their children of fobbing them off to a nursing home. They may initiate the move to make things easier for their children but secretly resent it.

The pending dilemma is how to balance elderly health care against that of the rest of the population. Should huge sums be spent on technology for the seriously ill who will probably die in the next months or year? In military parlance, we have a triage situation—weeding out the hopeless in order to concentrate on younger and healthier patients.

The most vigorous spokesman for triage is Dr. Daniel Callahan, an ethical philosopher at New York's Hastings Institute and author of the book *Setting Limits*. Opposing expensive and problematic treatment, he sees "no sense to improve medical care for the elderly while some 35 million Americans have no health insurance." He offers as evidence 25 to 35 percent of Medicare costs yearly going to 5 or 6 percent of the enrollees who will die within that year.[8]

Specifically, Callahan criticizes Medicare money spent on kidney dialysis. "It does not greatly increase life expectancy for its users (an average of only five years)," he argues, "and for most part, that gain is at the price of a doubtful or poor quality of life and an inability to achieve earlier levels of functioning." A seventy-six-year-old woman, for example, had a liver transplant at Pittsburgh's Presbyterian University Hospital in 1986 that cost $200,000 and she died four days later. "The infinite extension of life combined with an insatiable ambition to improve the health of the elderly is a recipe for monomania and bottomless spending," Callahan concludes.

Whether Callahan's position should be sanctioned or not, the most demanding necessity is that we give more options to the poor who are often denied health insurance and get far less attention from doctors and hospitals than the wealthy.

In the laws governing the evolution of an idea, we have reached a point where death with dignity could only become a national movement by arousing public debate. A highly publicized event came in December 1949, after the death of Mrs. Abbie C. Borotto, a fifty-nine-year-old New Hampshire housewife from a long and painful cancer. Hermann Sander, M.D., a Dartmouth Medical School graduate and popular resident of Candia, New Hampshire, who often sent no bills to poor patients, was arrested for injecting air into the patient's left arm and allegedly causing her death. He thus became the first physician in the country to stand trial for euthanasia or what the press called "mercy killing."

Sander explained to officials "There was no malice on my part" and that "ultimately my position will be vindicated." Although the trial hinged on whether the patient was already dead before injection, it became a testing ground for sentiment about death with dignity. The Vatican newspaper, *Observatore Romano,* proclaimed that mercy killing "injects the poison of atheism into the veins of society." In support of Sander, the minister of Manchester's First Congregational Church, preached, "If this man is felonious then so am I, for I have desired the time of suffering to be short." *Zion's Herald,* the country's oldest Methodist newspaper, urged that the Sander case should stimulate a change in the law.[9]

On March 8, 1950, the jury found Sander not guilty. One pivotal result was that three hundred prominent Britons, including the king's physician, signed a petition urging that a euthanasia clause be attached to the U.N.'s Declaration of Human Rights.

A shocking event was needed to coalesce nationwide opinion. It would come eventually on April 15, 1975, when Karen Ann Quinlan, adopted daughter of Joe and Julia Quinlan, went into a coma possibly as a result of combining alcohol and Valium.

At St. Clare's Hospital in Denville, New Jersey, the doctors pronounced Karen Ann's brain damage irreversible, but kept her alive on respirators, feeding tubes, and other technology. The Quinlans were Roman Catholics. Their priest, Father Tom Trapasso, backed by the local bishop, cited Pope Pius XII's ruling that extraordinary means did not have to be taken to prolong life. On July 31, the Quinlans asked their lawyer, Paul Armstrong, to petition the hospital to detach their daughter from all mechanical devices. When the hospital refused, Armstrong went to court.

The case received almost daily media attention, even overseas. Here was a once lovely woman, reduced not just to a vegetable, but to a convulsive mass of shrinking flesh that her parents visited daily. Before the New Jersey Supreme Court, their lawyer stressed the privacy rights of an individual, which had been protected by the U.S. Supreme Court in *Griswold v. Connecticut* in 1965 and *Roe v. Wade* in 1973. Her mother told the judges Karen Ann had always begged "don't ever let them keep me alive with extraordinary means." Her friends reported she had similar conversations with them. On March 31, 1976, the New Jersey court affirmed Karen Ann's privacy rights as "a matter of [her] self-determination," and ruled that "Ultimately there comes a point at which the individual's rights overcome the state's interests." Her father was made executor in charge of all medical decisions.[10]

The respirator was detached, and her parents moved Karen Ann to a nursing home. The Quinlans agreed not to remove the feeding tubes. Amazingly, she stayed in a coma another ten years, not dying until June 11, 1985. "Now we all have the right to die in peace and dignity," her mother commented. "A human tragedy and a bewildering legal riddle," the *Chicago Tribune* pronounced.[11]

Still, the case had little legal consequence outside New Jersey. Artificial feeding never became an issue until 1986 when the Massachusetts Supreme Court allowed Patrick Brophy to force New England Sinai Hospital to deny all food and water to his comatose son. Even then, the hospital evasively listed the cause of death as pneumonia.

It was not until 1990 that the U.S. Supreme Court began to define the rules for the death with dignity campaign. In January 1983, twenty-five-year-old Nancy Cruzan of Mt. Vernon, Missouri, lost control of her car, hit a tree, and probably stopped breathing for more than twelve minutes. After three and a half years at a rehabilitation center, doctors predicted she could stay in a coma for decades, and her parents asked that all technology be removed. The Missouri Supreme Court refused in a four to three decision. The Cruzans took the case to the U.S. Supreme Court. On June 25, 1990, the Court decreed that prior evidence of the patient's intent would now become mandatory. In a five to four vote, the Court stated that a patient could refuse unwanted medical treatment if there was "clear and convincing evidence" that the patient had previously announced this objective.[12]

Three of Cruzan's friends testified she had told them she never wanted to be kept alive on a respirator or feeding tubes. The Missouri attorney general bowed out of the case. Despite frenzied attempts by right-to-life groups to invade Cruzan's hospital room and feed her themselves, the Missouri court ordered the feeding tubes removed, and Cruzan died twelve days later, seven years after the accident. The strain may have been too much for her father, Joe Cruzan. On August 17, 1996, he hanged himself in his carport.

The progress of an idea always depends on a series of critical steps; in this case, the most crucial was the Court's prior evidence ruling. Consequently, death with dignity organizations now concentrated on promoting a living will and power of attorney, first suggested in 1967 by Luis Kutner, a founder of the Euthanasia Society of America. A further impetus in this direction came from the passage in Congress in 1990 of the Patient Self-Determination Act.[13]

The act requires that anyone entering a health care facility (where 80 percent of the population die) must be informed of the right to draw up a living will and appoint an agent with power of attorney, stipulating the kind of life-prolonging medical care the patient would accept or refuse. Many states accordingly drew up their own form of a living will. Patients could also use the form developed by Compassion in Dying and similar groups.

But what seemed like a critical step has fallen short of its promise. Only a small minority of patients sign living wills. Accepting the reality of our own death may be the final seal of our maturity, but most of us instinctively evade inevitability. Or we are convinced on entering a hospital that our prospects are too optimistic to require a living will. We often hesitate to give a husband, wife, or close relative the responsibility. We are troubled by the insistence of many doctors to retain decisions in their own hands and convinced that medical authority cannot be dealt with even through a legal document.

The greatest conflict between a patient and doctor in a serious illness has always been control of pain. Doctors have been loath to prescribe enough opiates such as morphine. They have long considered them habit-forming, a thesis not considered valid today. They have stuck to the conviction that pain is integral to dying, and consequently two-thirds of patients with advanced diseases spend the end of their life in pain, nausea, and depression.

Pain relief, known as palliative care, has finally penetrated the medical profession, largely through the work of Kathleen M. Foley, M.D., founder of the nation's first pain service at Sloan-Kettering Hospital in New York City in 1981. African-American cancer patients, the elderly in nursing homes, women, and children in particular lack adequate pain care. Although other countries recognized the problem—France, for example, legally provides pain medication paid for by the government—pain care in the United States is generally slighted by medical schools. There are only about nineteen palliative care fellowships in the country.

After the death with dignity campaign promoted the living will, its next objective was to educate potential members on three alternatives that gave them control of their own dying. The most traditional alternative is suicide, a word that has long disturbed society. It is not only an assault on the meaning of personhood, but on family members and friends who may suffer its consequences. Since humanity's drive for survival has been put in doubt, suicide has been condemned by most religions.

Family and friends often blame themselves for failing to detect suicidal signs. Although none of his associates could explain the suicide of the author, Jerzy Kosinski, in 1991, a long letter he had just written his wife shows that the decision was made carefully and rationally, possibly, as a friend explained, because he "loved life too much to live in it any other way than under the conditions he set."[14]

One state court has given a cognizant patient the right of implementing his own suicide. Larry McAfee, a thirty-three-year-old quadriplegic maimed and paralyzed as a result of a motorcycle accident, hired a lawyer to ask the Georgia Supreme Court the right to detach his respirator. On November 21, 1989, the court affirmed his right in a unanimous decision, based on federal and Georgia privacy laws, as long as he detached the respirator himself. McAfee never resorted to using the court's decision. He died of pneumonia on October 1, 1995.

Suicide by those dying painfully from AIDs has become increasingly common. Marty James described on national television in 1988 how he had helped at least eight patients commit suicide. They "had lived a very good life," he stated, and "wanted a very good death." In January 1992, James, who also had AIDs, committed suicide himself.[15]

Suicide must be recognized as an essential option in death with dignity. It gives people a choice, the possibility of leaving this earth at the moment we want. It gives us the chance to decide when our work is done and the things we desired have been achieved. It may be a decision that few of us will take, but should be free of legal obstructions such as penalties for a second person's participation. All laws criminalizing suicide in any way should be abolished.

The second alternative in the death with dignity campaign has been called "assisted suicide." It means that a doctor supplies a patient with a lethal dose, and the patient administers it himself. In its informal use, a doctor brings the dose to a patient's home (avoiding the legal blocks at a hospital, hospice, or nursing home) and indicates the amount of dosage that will produce death. The formal application of assisted suicide depends on a state law that sanctions it. Oregon is the only legal state so far, but the death with dignity campaign has begun to organize other states.

The third alternative has been called "voluntary active euthanasia." The doctor or other medical personnel actually administers the fatal dose orally or by injection. Although the Netherlands and other European countries have adopted this alternative, it remains suspect in the United States. The common fear is that a doctor may take a life without a patient's agreement, or that family members, driven by personal advantages such as inheritance, may try to influence a doctor.

In its evolutionary progress, the death with dignity campaign has now reached a point that demands leadership and organization. Although movements are mainly driven by social forces, individuals become essential in setting and reaching immediate objectives. In making suicide the center of national attention, Derek Humphry must be considered its first controversial proponent.[16]

Humphry was an English journalist, born on April 29, 1930, who came to the United States, and worked on the *Los Angeles Times*. When Jean, his wife of twenty-two years, was going through the pain of cancer and begged for relief, he helped her die in 1978 with a fatal dose of seconal and codeine. He wrote a book, *Jean's Way*, describing his help in her suicide, and was astounded at the outpouring of letters asking his advice. The public was finally making suicide a critical issue.

Humphry decided that an aggressive organization was needed to take over the moribund role of the Euthanasia Society. In 1980, he founded the Hemlock Society (named after the potion drunk by Socrates whose death was ordered by the Athenian state).

In 1991, Humphry wrote the book *Final Exit*, a handbook of suicide that would shock the country. It gave detailed descriptions of how to store up fatal doses from different doctors and gain cooperation from family and friends, the form of letters that should be left, and how to avoid autopsy, since insurance companies often refuse to pay off on suicide. As a backup, infallible technique, he recommended tying a plastic bag around the head to produce death by suffocation.

The book gathered an unexpectedly huge audience. It stayed on the *New York Times* best-seller list for eighteen weeks and, including foreign releases, sold more than a million copies. Yet, Hemlock Society membership lagged behind book sales. Neither Humphry nor anyone else at this moment had developed the skills of organizing a movement to change the laws.

Another individual whose book, *Last Wish*, furthered national debate in 1985 was Betty Rollin. She was an enticing woman, a well-known newscaster for national television in New York, which naturally brought readers to her finely wrought story about death. What Rollin gave the public was sensitivity, pathos, and a daughter's extreme devotion to her mother, who was stricken with ovarian cancer and begged Rollin to help her die when the pain became unbearable. Rollin and her husband secured the lethal drugs and took the risk of flouting the law by helping another person commit suicide.

Until now, only nonmedical people were building a mass base for the movement. Doctors generally had stayed well hidden. They were fearful of plunging into the most controversial issue of our time, tarnishing their reputations, and losing patients. They were especially worried that the slightest infringement of the law would result in the removal of their medical licenses.

This silence was resoundingly broken in 1991 by Timothy Quill, M.D., of the University of Rochester Medical School. He would bring the movement to its final stage by forcing the issue into state legislatures and launching a drive to pass state laws that would legalize death with dignity.[17]

Chapter 15

DEATH WITH DIGNITY WINS IN OREGON

It was an epochal date. On March 7, 1991, Timothy Quill, M.D., announced in the *New England Journal of Medicine* that he had done what a few doctors had been doing secretly for years. He told how he had helped put one of his longtime patients, Patricia Diane Trumbull, out of wrenching pain from cancer by giving her a lethal dose of barbiturates that she would administer herself. "She taught me that I can take small risks for people that I really know and care about," Quill wrote. His only regret was that neither he nor anyone else was with her when "she died alone."[1]

A prominent physician at Genesee Hospital as well as Rochester University Hospital, Quill had been particularly disturbed that four recent patients had died painful deaths. He admired Trumbull's struggle against alcoholism and depression and considered her a friend. The risks were obvious as soon as an autopsy was done on Trumbull's body. Quill had listed her death as "acute leukemia." Although Trumbull had insisted that he not be present at her death in an attempt to protect him, he was charged with manslaughter and tampering with the public record. Eventually, the grand jury decided not to prosecute him, and the New York State Health Department ruled that there had been no professional misconduct. Quill had broken through a barrier of medical silence, but it was doubtful that other doctors would follow him.

National attention soon turned to Jack Kevorkian, M.D. A skinny bespectacled pathologist, born in Michigan in 1928, he seemed determined to make a mockery of legal prohibitions against assisted suicide. His personal campaign became a theatrical drama.[2]

Janet Adkins, a fifty-four-year-old teacher from Portland, Oregon, was Kevorkian's first patient. Devoted to music and finally so destroyed by Alzheimer's disease that she could not strike the correct piano keys, Adkins had long been a member of the Hemlock Society. Her husband supported her decision, stating later she was "upset because she was losing her mind." In her last letter she wrote, "I do not want to put my family or myself through the horror of this terrible disease."

Although Adkins had chosen to act of her own free will, medical critics claimed that her disease was not advanced enough to warrant her death. Still, such decisions must always be subjective. Kevorkian made no medical diagnosis of this or any of the following cases—his degree in pathology hardly qualified him. On June 4, 1990, in Detroit, he simply supplied the death machine.

The machine (it went through numerous variations) usually consisted of three upside down bottles of a lethal gas with a dangling tube for inhalation and a string the patient would pull to activate it. For almost a decade Kevorkian helped people commit suicide—he would claim one hundred thirty but the number was undoubtedly less. One elderly woman even died in a Roman Catholic church in Detroit. Oakland County, Michigan, Prosecutor Richard Thompson would charge that one patient had no medical disease. Kevorkian's lawyer, however, called Thompson a headline hunter because he had lost in the recent Republican primary to a young opponent who announced he would not prosecute Kevorkian.

Michigan officials were determined to stop Kevorkian and, if possible, put him in jail. The first step was for the Michigan Board of Medicine to suspend Kevorkian's license indefinitely. A first-degree murder charge was dismissed in December 1990 by a judge who ruled that Michigan had no laws against assisted suicide. Although the *New York Times* called them "ghoulish stunts," jurors were obviously partial to assisted suicides. Kevorkian's trials resulted in three acquittals and one mistrial.

The case against Kevorkian reached a crisis on November 22, 1998, when he allowed CBS's popular television program "Sixty Minutes" to show him giving lethal drugs by injection to Thomas Youk, who was in advanced stages of Lou Gehrig's disease. Kevorkian, never bashful about publicity, insisted "I wanted a showdown." Youk's wife, Melody, stated, "I don't consider it murder. I consider it the way things should be done."

Following a Michigan law outlawing assisted suicide that took effect September 1, 1998, Oakland County Prosecutor David G. Gorcyca brought charges against Kevorkian for first-degree murder, criminal assistance to suicide, and delivery of a controlled substance, with the "Sixty Minutes" tape as principal evidence. It was the first trial that involved a killing by his own hand. Kevorkian insisted on defending himself and made constant legal errors. On March 26, 1999, he was convicted of second-degree murder and delivering a controlled substance. He was given a ten- to twenty-five-year sentence, and the Michigan Court of Appeals affirmed the conviction in 2001.

Geoffrey Fieger, Kevorkian's brash lawyer who would run a flamboyant but unsuccessful campaign for Michigan governor in 1998, told the *New York Times* that Kevorkian's work was not about the right to die but the "right to not suffer." Kevorkian, he insisted, "represents the idea at the core of what the Founding Fathers stood for: the right to determine your own destiny in the face of hopeless affliction."

Despite Kevorkian's tasteless methods and arrogance, he occupies a unique position in the evolutionary development of the idea of death with dignity. Every movement needs a tough and irreverent figure who can break through hypocrisy and community norms. Kevorkian did more than anyone else to concentrate the attention of the nation on assisted suicide. While some later reformers thought he harmed their cause, his peculiar form of dedication deserves recognition for heightening awareness of the ownership of our bodies.

The first contemporary campaign to change state laws preceded Kevorkian. In August 1972, Walter W. Sackett, Jr., M.D., admitted to the U.S. Senate Committee on Ageing that he had helped "hundreds of terminally ill patients" to die, and submitted a bill to the Florida legislature, of which he was a member, that amplified a 1967 bill on assisted suicide. The bill was ignored.[3]

Legislation in California didn't fare much better. In 1974, the mother-in-law of Barry Keene, a state assemblyman, suffered from painful cancer and could not get her doctors to limit treatment. Appalled, Keene drew up legislation whose preamble read: "Every person has the right to die without prolongation of life by medical means."[4]

It was attacked furiously by California's Medical Association, the Catholic Conference, and the Pro-Life Council. In an effort to compromise, Keene retitled the bill the "Natural Death Act." The bill was almost gutted, the remnants essentially providing for a living will. Passing both state senate and assembly, it was signed by Governor Jerry Brown on September 30, 1976.

Keene was determined to pass a more meaningful bill and went to the voters directly through the "initiative" process. Proposition 161 appeared on the ballot in November 1992. Keene had underestimated the huge cost of collecting the necessary signatures. Proponents collected only $215,000. Opponents, mainly the Catholic Church and Catholic groups, raised $2.8 million for a last-minute television and radio blitz. Although California is generally rated a liberal state, its expanding bloc of Hispanic voters, and even a growing Mormon population, were more concerned about jobs and education than death with dignity. The Southern end of the state was particularly conservative. Keene failed to build an organizing team, and his allies could not educate the voters in time. Proposition 161 was defeated by the convincing margin of 54 to 46 percent.

Washington was the first state with a scrupulously organized coalition behind Initiative 119 in November 1991. The historical progression of ideas had reached the point where a grassroots base could be put together by Washington Citizens for Death with Dignity and such allies as the Interfaith Clergy Coalition. The Initiative needed 150,000 signatures; more than 223,000 were collected. One million dollars were raised. Proponents were able to nullify the Washington Medical Association, which was so split that it decided to stay neutral.[5]

The Initiative employed a shrewd strategy. Washington had already become the second state to pass Living Will legislation. Instead of offering voters a new bill, Initiative 119 simply enlarged the previous Natural Death Act. It required two physicians to certify that a patient had less than six months to live. In its definition of terminal illness, it covered those in a "persistent vegetative state" or an "irreversible coma." It cited, among other provisions, the specific life-saving procedures that could be rejected. But now came the inflammatory section: The Initiative would "permit adult persons with terminal illness to request and receive aid in dying from their physicians, facilitating death."

If the vote had been taken in August, surveys showed the Initiative would have won. But opponents, such as Professor Albert R. Jansen of the University of Washington, stressed that the Initiative would "legalize active euthanasia." The Catholic Church countered with massive television and radio spots, claiming there was no regulatory oversight, no requirement for psychological evaluation. "Do you want your doctor deciding . . . when you deserve to die?" demanded Leon R. Kass, M.D., of the University of Chicago. Opponents produced a survey of three hundred Dutch doctors (never documented) that supposedly found that 40 percent of euthanasia deaths were done without the patient's request.

A Protestant clergyman, Anthony B. Robinson, in the liberal *Christian Century* wrote that medical euthanasia will "heighten our tendency to isolate the suffering and dying." Even the ethicist Daniel Callahan, who, as we have seen, supported triage, opposed the Initiative, claiming "Our duty to relieve suffering cannot justify the introduction of new evils into society."

The Initiative leadership had made a serious error by leaping ahead of public opinion. Under a barrage of Catholic media money and growing fears that doctors would exert far more control than words indicated, Initiative 119 went down to defeat by the surprising margin of 54 to 46 percent.

The Washington disaster spurred the movement to look for new strategies. The evolution of an idea rarely moves in a direct line. Movements may have to experiment with what works best, whether to concentrate on legislatures, courts, or building a base of voters. As an array of groups fused into Compassion in Dying, Oregon, now the most aggressive state, turned to the federal courts to overthrow a ban on assisted suicide that had been on the books since 1854.

In Compassion's case in U.S. District Court in Seattle, Judge Barbara Rothstein ruled on May 4, 1994, that the ban violated the Fourteenth Amendment clause against state interference with individual liberty. She quoted from the U.S. Supreme Court's ringing words in *Planned Parenthood v. Casey*: "At the heart of liberty is the right to define one's own concept of existence, of meaning, of the universe, and of the mysteries of human life." She concluded: "Like the abortion decision, the decision of a terminally ill person to end his or her life 'involves the most intimate and personal choice a person can make in a lifetime'" and constitutes a "choice central to personal dignity and autonomy."[6] Compassion's credo had been brilliantly defined and affirmed later by the U.S. Court of Appeals. Still, it would be considerably diluted by the U.S. Supreme Court.

Compassion, with affiliates around the country, now became the central force in the death with dignity campaign. Its objectives were sweeping. It not only aimed to pass a new Oregon law, but its free services covered everything from hospice care to pain management to support for those in the final stages of illness. It adopted an approach that appealed to all sectors of society. "We have demonstrated," announced Barbara Coombs Lee, its president, "that the interests of individual patients in a death of their own choosing and the larger interests of society in preventing errors and abuse can both be protected."[7]

When William Bergman, an eighty-five-year-old Californian with terminal lung cancer, was denied adequate pain care at Eden Medical Center, his widow and Compassion's lawyer, Kathryn Tucker, went to court. The jury decided that treatment by Bergman's doctor constituted reckless neglect of the elderly and awarded a judgment of $1.5 million.

Barbara Coombs Lee, a striking fifty-six-year-old woman with two grown children and three teenagers, graduated from Vassar and the Cornell University School of Nursing. She grew up near Chicago and moved to Oregon in 1972. After twenty-five years as a medical assistant, she got her law degree from Lewis and Clark University in 1986 and served as counsel to the U.S. Senate Health Care Committee.

Personal motivation is a dominant factor in influencing an individual to assume leadership of a movement. Lee drew her motivation from her friend, Oregon State Senator Frank Roberts, whose wife Barbara Roberts became governor. Although Roberts had terminal prostate cancer and was finally restricted to a wheelchair, he introduced pioneering bills on assisted suicide in 1987, 1989, and 1991. The first two bills didn't even get a hearing. The third got a hearing but languished in committee.

An avid bird-watcher who kept a wood carving of a red-tailed hawk on his desk, Roberts lay dying in 1993 when his wife told him, "It's time to let go, Frank. You can fly like a hawk, float on the air." As her tribute to Roberts, Lee helped draft the assisted-suicide law, which was approved in Oregon on November 8, 1994. A momentous advance, it was the first such law in the country.

Lee was a skilled organizer. She recruited and trained local leadership throughout the state. She knew how to raise money—George Soros contributed. Her coalition of supporting groups centered on religions such as United Church of Christ and United Methodist Church.

Above all, Compassion grasped the cause of failure in Washington state and changed strategy completely. It wanted the issue to be sharply defined for the broadest audience. Instead of allowing physicians to put a patient to death, which was the main source of contention in Washington, Measure 16 in Oregon gave all the power to the patient. Only the patient could request the fatal dose from the doctor and take it alone without the doctor's presence. Medical euthanasia was thus eliminated.[8]

Further, Measure 16 contained an array of safeguards. A patient had to make two oral and one written request. A doctor had to guarantee the patient had only six months to live, and that guarantee had to be approved by a second doctor. A fifteen-day waiting period gave the patient a chance to change his or her mind. If there was a hint of depression, the patient had to go for psychological counseling. Health care providers could refuse to participate and were immune from criminal liability. Patients had to be residents of Oregon; doctors had to be licensed in Oregon.

In a tempestuous campaign, the opposition, mainly Catholic, spent $1.5 million. Compassion spent $600,000. Opposition arguments stressed that, "Life and death rightfully should be left in the hands of God." Compassion countered that the Catholic Church was trying "to impose their own unique theological argument on the entire state."

Insisting that Measure 16 would reinforce the view that dying people are an unnecessary burden, the opposition deluged the public with special claims. Fifty percent of Oregon doctors, they announced, cannot accurately predict when a patient will die. Fred Stickel, Catholic publisher of the *Oregonian*, produced such inflammatory headlines as "Pills Don't Work" and "Dutch Researcher Warns of Lingering Deaths." The claim that fatal doses might not be quickly effective was based on no solid evidence.

Oregon voters approved Measure 16 by the slim margin of 51 to 49 percent. "The people want to govern their own lives, not let the church or government decide for them," declared the wife of Judge Irving Steinbok, who had managed to get a fatal dosage for her husband who died before using it. "All we did was legalize that which was covert," explained Barbara Coombs Lee. "I believe an individual should have control," proclaimed Oregon Governor John Kitzhaber, a physician.

But before the new law could take effect, the opposition tied it up in three years of judicial and legislative wrangling. The state legislature forced a second vote on the same referendum that would cost $1 million. But polls showed that retention of the new law had gained support. On November 4, 1997, Oregon voters approved the law again by a decisive 60 percent. Oregon became the first area in the world with assisted suicide, proving in the words of Timothy Quill, M.D., that people "don't want to be told what they can or cannot do with their own death."[9]

In March 1998, an elderly woman who had been struggling against breast cancer for twenty-two years died in her sleep thirty minutes after taking the fatal dose. As the first person to be treated under the new law, she had made a tape beforehand, saying, "I'm looking forward to it."

Despite threats by opponents that Oregon would be known as a killing field, the remarkable outcome was that few took advantage of the law. In 1998, sixteen people chose to die under its provisions. In 1999 and 2000, there were twenty-seven cases each year, a total of 91 by 2002. All gave as their motivation a loss of autonomy. Cancer was the prime illness followed by heart disease. All were Caucasian; males and females were almost evenly split. Two volunteer case workers from Compassion were present at each death. State officials ruled that Medicaid patients would be covered.

As death with dignity became a national issue comparable to abortion, Congressional conservatives were determined to crush the Oregon law and what they called a "culture of death." Oklahoma Senator Don Nickles and Illinois Representative Henry Hyde, both Republicans, introduced bills neatly disguised under the title of "Pain Relief Promotion Act." The basic intent, however, was to ban the use by doctors of drugs that could hasten death. Violations could bring doctors up to twenty years in jail. The bill never reached a vote in the Senate.

The Bush administration, undoubtedly as a sop to its right-wing base, now resorted to an unprecedented approach. Since it couldn't get a bill through Congress, it would seek the same end by executive order. On November 6, 2001, Attorney General John Ashcroft, supposedly busy with countering terrorism, took the time to gut the Oregon law by ordering the Drug Enforcement Agency to ban doctors from giving lethal doses of federally controlled drugs.[10]

Ashcroft's order pulverized Oregon officials. The states' whole Congressional delegation (except for Republican Senator Gordon Smith) denounced it. Governor Kitzhaber labeled it an "unprecedented invasion" of Oregon's ability to regulate medical practices. U.S. Senator Ron Wyden, who significantly had opposed the new law, declared that Ashcroft's order would "toss the ballots of Oregonians into the trash can." The previous attorney general, Janet Reno, had ruled that the precedent Ashcroft was drawing on only applied to drug trafficking and was not intended to cover an assisted-suicide law. A *New York Times* editorial concluded that the Drug Enforcement Agency "has no right to substitute its own judgment for the judgment of Oregon voters."

Oregon's Attorney General, Hardy Myers, immediately went into federal court to seek a stay, arguing that Ashcroft's ban was unconstitutional because it interfered with Oregon's supervision of its medical and health care systems.

"Will federal agents now second-guess doctors who prescribe potential pain killers?" demanded a *Chicago Tribune* editorial. James Romney, a high school principal with Lou Gehrig's disease complained, "It took away all my sense of liberty." On November 8, 2001, Judge Robert E. Jones in U.S. District Court issued a stay of Ashcroft's order, allowing patients to be treated in the meantime. On April 17, 2002, Judge Jones overthrew the ban.

Ashcroft's action was a supreme irony. One of the main themes of Bush's election campaign was to diminish the role of the federal government and return responsibility to the states. But Oregon's assisted-suicide law had been approved by the voters in two elections and signed by the governor. Few laws had received such a popular mandate. Yet, the Bush administration was seeking to overturn a significant instance of states' rights.

The U.S. Supreme Court now gave its imprimatur to death with dignity state campaigns. Compassion in Dying, as we have seen, had won its case against Washington state's ban on assisted suicide with the Rothstein decision in U.S. District Court and the Reinhardt decision in Appeals Court. On June 26, 1997, the Supreme Court overthrew the lower courts by reversing similar decisions in Washington state and New York. It is a reasonable assumption that the Court did not want to entangle itself with an even more volcanic issue than it had done with abortion in *Roe v. Wade*. Still, the Court gave a sizable boost to death with dignity by concluding that its decision "permits this debate to continue, as it should in a democratic society." The campaign, consequently, would spread to other states.[11]

Legislative actions would fail in Maine, Idaho, and elsewhere. A judicial test, *Sampson & Doe v. State of Alaska,* was defeated in the Alaska courts. Michigan undertook a determined campaign to win a PAS law (Physicians Assisted Suicide). The organizing group, Merian's

Friends, collected 261,000 signatures to get on the ballot. Early polls showed 59 percent of voters in favor. But money, as always, reversed the tide. Opponents spent $5 million compared to only $1 million for proponents. The Michigan Republican Party joined Catholic and right-to-life factions in bitter attacks. Kevorkian didn't help by criticizing the bureaucratic strictures of the bill. On November 3, 1998, it was defeated by a resounding two to one margin.

Meanwhile, assisted-suicide laws in other countries stimulated debate. Switzerland has no formal law, but almost never prosecutes a doctor for assisted suicide. Surprisingly, in the Catholic country of Colombia, the high Constitutional Court ruled that no one should be penalized for assisting the dying of a competent and terminally ill adult who "suffered terrible pain incompatible with his idea of dignity." After an Australian survey showed that one in three general surgeons gave excess pain medication to dying patients, the Superior Court of Western Australia acquitted a doctor of willfully murdering a patient with kidney cancer.[12]

The Netherlands, however, became the first country in the world to pass a comprehensive law. The practice of assisted suicide had actually been going on unofficially for years and was even shown on public television in 1994. Catholics (except for a few bishops) and Protestants worked in partnership. Polls showed that about 80 per cent of the public and medical profession wanted a law. The National Association for Voluntary Euthanasia claimed 100,000 members in a country with a population of 15 million. "We don't want something of this importance to go on underground," announced Rob Jonquiere, its director. On November 28, 2000, the Dutch Parliament approved a euthanasia bill, which became law in 2002.[13] A similar law in Belgium was passed shortly afterwards.

Its basic feature was that the patient's request must be voluntary. The doctor, confirmed by a second doctor, must be assured of "unremitting pain and unbearable suffering" and that the patient found no other acceptable alternative. A doctor was not accountable to a prosecutor but to a panel of peers. It must be stressed that a doctor could not only supply a fatal dosage, as in Oregon, but that the doctor himself would often put the patient to death. Thus the Dutch law must be classified as euthanasia. And it had vague areas that would soon be tested in court. Edward Brongersma, a former senator, had no serious physical or psychological illness; he just complained of a "pointless and empty existence." When his doctor was brought to court, he was found guilty but given no jail sentence since the court found he had "acted out of compassion" for his patient.

Another attempt to legislate death with dignity was made in California in 1999. The bill's sponsor was assemblywoman Dion Aroner from Berkeley. A 1966 graduate of the University of California at Berkeley, she had been a social worker and union organizer for five years and an aide to a member of the County Board of Supervisors for twenty-five years before being elected to the legislature herself in 1996. Her interest in assisted suicide was intensely personal. Without a California law, her mother, who had Alzheimer's disease, had to refuse food and water to starve herself to death. Aroner's aunt committed suicide at age eighty, and her mother's brother undertook a form of suicide by pulling all the tubes and technology from his body that doctors insisted he needed.[14]

Aroner's bill was almost an exact duplicate of Oregon's. There were more Catholics in the legislature now than in Barney Keene's time. The governor was a converted Catholic. Aroner was unable to build an organizational coalition and had little money. "If we'd had more money, we could have won," she insists. Instead, when her count showed almost certain defeat in the assembly, she let the bill languish on the floor.

Although the Maine referendum lost by only 51.5 to 48.5 percent, it seems reasonable to conclude that Oregon may temporarily remain the only state in the country with an assisted-suicide law. This may seem to refute my historical proposition, particularly true in birth control and abortion rights, that one breakthrough invariably leads to similar breakthroughs elsewhere.

Yet, assisted suicide remains at a considerable disadvantage. It lacks the essential base in the women's movement that birth control and abortion rights have. It lacks the big money that flows easily to those causes. Since most people avoid thinking about dying, it lacks huge national organizations to drive state campaigns despite the growth of Compassion in Dying and Death with Dignity National Center. If Maine, Michigan, and Washington state can duplicate the organizing and fund-raising of Oregon, they are the logical sites of coming success. The historical position on breakthroughs that we have developed may simply have been postponed.

Assisted suicide is part of the process of taking charge of our own death and of making sense of the whole of our lives. We want to leave this earth satisfied and complete. Anything that gives us meaning gives us that much more power over dying. "After one has lived a life of meaning," concludes Robert N. Butler, M.D., professor of geriatrics at Mt. Sinai Medical School in New York City, "death may lose its terror. For what we fear most is not really death but a meaningless and absurd life."[15]

Chapter 16
SUM-UP

If ideas rule society, they also show the fragility of American society. We must define a country whose divisions become deeper and more inexplicable. We look at a picture in the newspapers of Christ Community Church in Alamogordo, New Mexico, where books of Harry Potter and Shakespeare are burned publicly after the minister calls them a "satanic deception." Is this Germany under Hitler? Can a minister in 2001 be re-creating the Salem witch trials? We wonder how America can produce such an absurdity.

But absurdity is all around us. Pat Robertson of the Christian Coalition blames the federal courts, pornography, abortion rights and church-state separation for angering God so blatantly that he blames us for the terrorism of September 11.

Extremists dig up endless arguments to destroy church-state separation, a bedrock of the Founding Fathers, and to prove that Thomas Jefferson's letter of January 1, 1802, defining the "wall of separation between Church and State," is a fraud. They take over school boards to eliminate Darwin's theories from textbooks. They try to force school prayer into classrooms despite federal court prohibitions. They have taken over the largest Protestant denomination in the country, the Southern Baptist Convention, and are penetrating the Episcopal, United Methodist, and Presbyterian Churches.

We must deal with a divided country where ideas, that once seemed immutable, are being shredded; where one group has made everyone accept permanent warfare as the unshakable logic of our times. Buoyed by the election of President Bush whose campaign depended on right-wing views, an estimated 17 percent of the electorate is determined to stamp its programs on the majority.

Extremists have been promoting an idea that may dominate the nation's direction. With the popularity of Bush's invasion of Afghanistan, the president's war on terrorism could be extended to Iraq, the Philippines, or Indonesia in an effort to eradicate Muslim militants. Extremists say that we are the number one world power. Why shouldn't we rule the world as the French did under Napoleon and the British did under Queen Victoria? We have dethroned communism. We must now install our own form of American empire.

Marxism may have been the theoretical engine of world politics for a hundred years, but it is now in tatters. It survives piecemeal in China, where the government struggles to balance memories of Mao with its new brand of capitalism. It maintains a symbolic status in Vietnam, in an isolated Cuba, and in a few rebel bands in Latin America. In the United States, Marxism retains a handful of disciples on college campuses.

Even moderate types of democratic socialism, once the mainstay of the European left, have been decimated at the polls or have withered away. The kibbutzim in Israel, backbone of the country during the Arab-Israel war of 1948, are becoming antique memorials. The few remaining collectives depend on manufacturing plants rather than on agriculture.

As the revolutionary zeal of Marxism has ebbed, American dominance has produced counterforces against new ideas. We no longer live in an ambience that nurtures progress such as the civil rights and women's movements of the 1960s. The groundswell for burgeoning movements has been blocked by threats of terrorism. How much of the public can be rallied around the problem of a depleted ozone layer? Although stem cells have the potential for alleviating

Alzheimer's and other critical diseases, President Bush's strictures on such research roused little popular protest.

There is a desperate need for ideas that will grip the public's imagination, ideas like the G.I. Bill of Rights, which educated millions of servicemen and were integral to the economic boom after World War II. We need ideas that will bring more voters to the polls. We need ideas that will stir the campuses to political and social action. We need ideas that will tap the unrest of political dissidents and produce more provocative legislation such as the death with dignity act in Oregon.

Above all, we need ideas that will strengthen the relationships between Americans. As the country moves quickly toward the point where Hispanic, African-Americans, and other ethnic groups dominate the population, we must give them an equal share of America's rewards. The overwhelming problem today is that a rising percentage of income is going to a small slice of the richest Americans ($1,016 million annually to the top 1 percent), while most of the middle class ($45,000 income annually) and the poor are benefiting little. President Bush only accentuates the problem with tax cuts for the wealthy.

Who is going to demand that the idea of equal opportunity must become the guiding code for America's future? Who is going to legislate a guarantee that minorities get justice not just in education but in jobs and paychecks? It cannot come too soon. For, when minority voters rule the legislatures and become obsessed with their economic plight, their vengeance may be brutal.

I have tried to prove the power of ideas in shaping our society. I have tried to show that ideas are the poetry of our existence. They sing in our blood. They captivate our minds. Ideas have propelled this country since the Constitutional Convention first codified the most portentous collection of them in human history. America depends as much on ideas as on the products of its factories. The basic idea of our culture is that the individual is no longer a pawn in the grip of governments or nature's God, but a citizen who now has the power and knowledge to control his or her own destiny. Ideas give us the machinery for our hopes and aims. If we ever lose this conviction, the country will stagnate.

NOTES

Introduction

1. Schlesinger in obituary of Berlin. "A Great Man in a Grim Time," *New York Times,* November 10, 1997.

Chapter 1

1. Norman E. Himes, *Medical History of Contraception* (Baltimore: Williams & Wilkens, Co., 1936), 59, 63, 87.

2. J. G. C. Blacker, "Social Ambitions of the Bourgeois in Eighteenth Century France," *Population Studies* 11, no. 1 (July 1957): 46

3. Blacker, "Social Ambitions," 85–86; Charles S. Lobingier, "Napoleon Centenary's Legal Significance," *American Law Review* 55 (January–February 1921): 665; Bernard Schwartz, *The Code Napoleon and the Common Law World* (New York: New York University Press, 1956), 7, 39, 140; Joseph J. Spengler, *France Faces Depopulation* (Durham, N.C.: Duke University Press, 1979) 65, 148.

4. Shirley Green, *The Curious History of Contraception* (London: Ebury Press, 1971) 79, 82, 86, 91.

5. Sripati Chandrasekhar, *A Dirty, Filthy Book* (Berkeley: University of California Press, 1981) 17, 24.

6. Eugene Quay, "Justifiable Abortion—Medical and Legal Foundations," *The Georgetown Law Journal* 49, no. 3 (spring 1961): 414, 415, 419, 425; Edvard Westermarck, *Origin and Development of Moral Ideas*, vol. 1, 2d ed. (London: Macmillan & Co., Ltd., 1924), 54.

7. 43 George 3, c. 58 (Ellenborough Act) in *A Collection of the Public General Statutes Passed in the 43rd Year of His Majesty King George III* (London: George Eyre & Andrew Strahan, 1903); Lord Ellenborough

Act, Select Committee Laws, Parliamentary Session Papers, vol. 8 (London, 1819), 43.

8. William L. Langer, "Europe's Initial Population Explosion," *American Historical Review* 69 (October 1963).

9. Graham Wallas, *Life of Francis Place* (Burt Franklin, N.Y., 1951), 4, 10, 19, 30, 38.

10. *London Times,* 19 June 1877, 11; Hypatia Bradlaugh Bonner, *Charles Bradlaugh* (London: T. Fisher Unwin, 1908), 247.

11. Himes, *Medical History,* 227.

12. David Tribe, *President Charles Bradlaugh, M.P.* (London: Elek Books, 1971), 41; Geoffrey West, *Mrs. Annie Besant* (London: Gerald Howe, Ltd., 1927), 34.

13. Adolphe S. Headingly, *Biography of Charles Bradlaugh* (London: Remington & Co., 1880), 32.

14. Centenary Committee, *Champion of Liberty: Charles Bradlaugh* (London: C. A. Watts & Co., 1933), 29, 44.

15. *Essex Standard* quoted in Gertrude Marvin Williams, *The Passionate Pilgrim: A Life of Annie Besant* (New York: Coward-McCann, 1931), 96.

16. Arthur H. Nethercot, *The First Five Lives of Annie Besant* (Chicago: University of Chicago Press, 1960), 132.

17. Centenary Committee, *Champion of Liberty,* 46; Nethercot, *First Five Lives,* 236.

Chapter 2

1. G. W. Foote, *Mr. Bradlaugh's Trial* (London: Charles Watt, 1877), 8.

2. Bonner, *Charles Bradlaugh,* 17.

3. Shirley Green, *The Curious History of Contraception* (London: Ebury Press, 1971), 164; *In the High Court of Justice: Queen's Bench Division, June 18, 1877. The Queen v. Charles Bradlaugh and Annie Besant* (London: Forethought Publishing Co., 1877).

4. *In the High Court of Justice: The Queen v. Bradlaugh,* 52–53.

5. *London Times,* 19 June 1877, 11.

6. Annie Besant, *Charles Bradlaugh: A Character Sketch* (Madras: Theosophical Publishing House, 1941), 52.

7. Charles Bradlaugh, "Poverty and Its Effect on the Political Condition of the People," pamphlet (London, 1863).

8. J. A. Banks and Olive Banks, "The Bradlaugh-Besant Trial and English Newspapers," *Population Studies* 3, no. 1 (July 1954).

9. Bonner, *Charles Bradlaugh,* 24.

10. *Reynolds Newspaper,* 22 July 1877, 1.

11. Green, *Curious History,* 22, 23; Lord Sydenham, "Dame Mary Scharlieb," *Health and Empire* 5 (1930): 262–64.

12. Annie Besant, *The Laws of Population: Its Bearing on Human Conduct and Morals* (London: Free Thought Publishing Co., 1877), 15.

13. This and the following two paragraphs are based on a unique study by Ethel Elderton, *Report on the English Birthrate* (London: University of London, 1914); Arthur Newsholme et al., "Decline of Human Fertility in the United Kingdom," *Royal Statistical Society* (March 1906): 44–137.

Chapter 3

This chapter is based on three years of interviewing Margaret Sanger (1952–1954) for my biography of her: *Margaret Sanger and the Fight for Birth Control* (New York: Doubleday, 1955). About one hundred original letters are housed at the Houghton Library, Harvard University. Copies are at the Margaret Sanger Project, New York University, 53 Washington Square South. Notebooks and other materials are at Widener Library, Harvard, and at the Radcliffe Institute for Advanced Study, Schlesinger Library, Harvard.

1. Emma Goldman's prior speeches on family limitation are covered in photograph and text in Roger A. Bruns, *The Damndest Radical* (Chicago: University of Illinois Press, 1987), 187–88; "Photo" following p. 152.

2. Eugene Quay, "Justifiable Abortion—Medical and Legal Foundation," *The Georgetown Law Journal* 49, no. 3 (spring 1961): 395–538.

3. Annual Reports of the President and Treasurer of Harvard College, 1901–1902 (Cambridge: Harvard University, 1903), 31–32; Theodore Roosevelt, "Race Decadence," *Outlook* (April 8, 1911): 765.

4. Mabel Dodge Luhan, *Movers and Shakers* (New Mexico: University Press, 1985), 69–71.

Chapter 4

As in chapter 3, chapter 4 is based on my three years interviewing Margaret Sanger and friends and associates essential to her work. Letters between us and other documents are at libraries listed in chapter 3 notes.

1. Elderton, *Report on the English Birthrate,* 199.
2. Opponents of Margaret Sanger concentrated their assaults on her links to the eugenics movement. This happened because of her desperation for any allies at that difficult time and possibly because mentors like Dr. Drysdale were sympathetic to eugenics. So much of her writing is devoted to bolstering the happiness of the poor that it is illogical to think she wanted to eliminate the most vulnerable members. Within a few years she severed all ties to eugenics.

Chapter 5

As in chapter 3 and 4, this chapter is largely based on three years of interviewing Margaret Sanger and friends and associates. Letters and documents housed in libraries are listed in chapter 3.

The development of the birth control pill is described in my article for the *New York Times Magazine*, April 10, 1966. Interviews were conducted with Gregory Pincus, Ph.D., and M. C. Chang, Ph.D., and their associates and families at Worcester Foundation for Experimental Biology in Massachusetts and with Dr. John Rock and associates at the Rock Reproduction Clinic in Brookline, Massachusetts. Katherine McCormick and officials at the Population Council, New York City, and at test sites were also interviewed.

1. The increasing safety of the birth control pill has mainly stemmed from the writing and testimony of Barbara Seaman.
2. These and other statistics in the chapter supplied by Stanley Henshaw, Ph.D., of EngenderHealth, New York City.
3. For this and the following two paragraphs, see *Let Every Child Be Wanted* (Westport, Conn.: Auburn House, 1999) by Philip D. Harvey, where he describes his remarkable work of marketing contraceptives around the world.

4. An analysis of the history of *Griswold v. Connecticut* is told superbly in David J. Garrow's book *Liberty and Sexuality* (New York: Macmillan Publishing Co., 1994).
5. *Griswold v. Connecticut*, 381 U.S. 479 (1965) and *Roe v. Wade*, 410 U.S. 113 (1973)

Chapter 6

The material in this chapter is drawn from my books *Abortion* (1966), *Abortion II* (1973), *RU 486* (1991), and *A Private Matter* (1995) and from many articles and editorials for the *New York Times, The Nation*, and other magazines. Material also comes form my personal experiences as founding chair of the National Abortion Rights Action League (1969–1975) and president of Abortion Rights Mobilization (1975–present). I have also corroborated my memory by interviewing veterans such as Dr. Lonny Myers, Ruth Smith, and Percy Sutton.

1. An excellent summary of the history of abortion laws is in Eugene Quay, "Justifiable Abortion—Medical and Legal Foundations," *The Georgetown Law Journal* 49, no. 3 (spring 1961): 395–538. See also Cyril C. Means, Jr., "The Law of New York Concerning Abortion and the Status of the Foetus," *New York Law Forum* (fall 1968): 493–98.
2. The number of abortions in the United States before legalization has always been debated. From my own study of thousands of obstetrician-gynecologists, made with the help of Dr. William Ober, I lean toward a figure of about a million annually.
3. *United States v. Vuitch*, 402 U.S. 62 (1971)

Chapter 7

As in chapter 6, material in chapter 7 is drawn from my books and articles on abortion rights mentioned in the previous chapter's notes and my personal involvement in the movement.

1. *Doe v. Bolton*, 410 U.S. 179 (1973)

Chapter 8

1. The Global Gag Rule is described in a pamphlet issued by Population Action International of Washington, D.C., in August 2001.

2. *Church and State*, March 2000, 10.

3. Statistics on women's employment and education in this and the following paragraphs are drawn from AARP publications: Heather Nawrocki and Steven R. Gregory, *Across the States 2000* (Washington, D.C., 2000); "Older Americans 2000," Indicator 1, Appendix A; Indicator 25; Indicator 1; *Health Affairs: The Policy Journal of the Health Sphere 20*, no. 2 (March 2001).

4. Maria Vullo argued the rehearing: *Planned Parenthood of the Columbia/Willamette, Inc., et al., v. American Coalition of Life Activists, et al.*, U.S. Court of Appeals, ninth circuit, no. 99-35320, April 11, 2001.

5. Newspaper stories describing the RU 486 challenge include: *New York Times*, 2 July 1992, A-12 and 15 July 1992, A-1; *Newsday*, 2 July 1992, 6; *USA Today*, 2 July 1992, 3-A; *Washington Post*, 15 July 1992, A-1; *Salt Lake Tribune*, 15 November 1992, A-1.

6. Among medical papers reporting on our work area: Eric Schaff et al., "Vaginal Misoprostol Administered 1, 2, and 3 Days after Mifepristone for Early Medical Abortion," *Journal of the American Medical Association* 284 (2000): 1948–51.

7. Advertisement that appeared in the *New York Times*, 4 April 2001, A-15.

8. For this and the following two paragraphs, see *Emergency Contraception 101* (New York: NARAL/NY Foundation, 2001); Kathryn Kolbert, *Improving Access to Reproductive Health Services for Teenagers* (New York: Open Society Institute, 2001).

9. *Church and State*, March 2000, 10; Clara S. Haignere, Rachel Gold, and Heather J. McDaniel, "Adolescent Abstinence and Condom Use," *Health Education and Behavior* 26, no. 1 (February 1999): 43–54.

10. "60 Minutes" on CBS, June 2, 1996; *New York Times* editorials, 1 April 1996, A-17, and 25 September 1999, A-14.

11. The originals of the letters sent to me by women pleading for abortion before legalization are housed at the Schlesinger Library, Radcliffe. Many letters were destroyed by me when I as summoned to a Bronx grand jury.

Chapter 9

This chapter is based on documents from and interviews with the staff of EngenderHealth in New York City, the dominant U.S. agency in the field. Paul Henshaw and Mike Klitsch have always been particularly helpful.

The chapter is also based on my years as an officer and board member of the organization and on my book *Foolproof Birth Control: Male and Female Sterilization* (Boston: Beacon Press, 1972), now partly outdated. Especially useful is the pamphlet "Sterilization," ACOG Technical Bulletin no. 222 (April 1996).

1. *Buck v. Bell,* 274 U.S. 200 (1927).
2. The remarkable work of Hugh Moore is summarized in my book *Breeding Ourselves to Death* (New York: Ballantine Books, 1971), reprinted by Negative Population Growth, Washington, D.C.
3. *New York Times,* December 10, 2002, F5

Chapter 10

This chapter is based on my long friendship with Betty Friedan and close association with her in the women's movement, starting in 1942 and intensifying as she worked on *The Feminine Mystique*, when we had nearby desks at the New York Pubic Library. I also talked with some of her former associates, who prefer not to be named.

Friedan has had frequent clashes with the women's movement, partly due to personality, partly due to issues. Although I have generally supported her on issues, I have regretted her increasing conservatism along with most feminist leaders. Yet, the daring of her ideas and her ability to make them a reality, no matter how many egos she punctured, guarantee her place in history.

Her autobiography *Life So Far* (New York: Simon & Schuster, 2000) often lacks objectivity, particularly with regard to the abortion rights movement where she was not always pivotal in debate and action. Two other books should be consulted concerning the development of her ideas: Daniel Horowitz, *Betty Friedan and the Making of the Feminine Mystique* (Amherst: University of Massachusetts Press, 1998) and Judith Hennessee, *Betty Friedan* (New York: Random House, 1999).

Chapter 11

1. Marguerite Michaels, "Myth of the Gender Gap," *Parade* (March 4, 1984), 4–5.
2. On Red Stockings, see Robin Morgan, ed., *Sisterhood Is Powerful* (New York: Vintage Books, 1970), 534. On combat, see Barbara Brown et al., "The Equal Rights Amendment," *Yale Law Journal* 80 (1971): 890.
3. Article V of the Constitution provides for amendments in any one of four ways.
4. On man's responsibility, see Jane O'Reilly, "The Big Time Players," *Ms. Magazine* (January 1983), 37. On Schlafly for this and the following paragraph, see Carol Felsenthal, *The Sweetheart of the Silent Majority* (Garden City, N.Y.: Doubleday, 1981), xi, 25, 118, 245, 273.
5. On Smathers, see Sharon Whitney, *The Equal Rights Amendment* (New York: Franklin Watts, 1984), 82.
6. Mary Frances Berry, *Why the ERA Failed* (Bloomington, In.: Indiana University Press, 1986), 72.
7. Schlafly Report 5, no. 7 (February 1972): 3–4.
8. Schlafly on combat: Yet, 73 percent of the American public supported the ERA by 1982, according to a Lou Harris poll. See Lawrence Lader, *Politics, Power, and the Church* (New York: Macmillan Publishing Co., 1987).
9. *Ensign*, January 1974, 7; *Miami Herald*, 20 April 1980, 1.
10. Insurance lobby in NOW research files, Washington, D.C., and NOW advertisement in the *New York Times*, 3 June 1982.

Chapter 12

1. For African-Americans in the Civil War, see Lawrence Lader, *The Bold Brahmins: New England's War Against Slavery* (New York: E.P. Dutton & Co., 1961), 277–92, which describes the 54th Massachusetts black regiment and 180,000 black troops in the Army (37,000 killed, wounded, or missing) and almost 30,000 in the Navy.
2. Interview with E. D. Nixon and Virginia F. Durr.
3. Helen Fuller, "We the People of Alabama," *New Republic* (June 5, 1961), 21–23. Interviews with Julian Bond and Esther Jackson.

4. Robert F. Williams, "Can Negroes Afford to Be Pacified?," *Liberation* (September 1959), 4–7; George Anne Geyer, "Odyssey of Robert Williams," *New Republic* (March 20, 1971), 15–17. Interviews with John Gerassi and Conrad Lynn.

5. *Nashville Banner*, 17 February 1964.

6. On Lewis, see Margaret Long, "March on Washington," *New South* (September 1963), 3–19 and Malcolm X (with Alex Haley), *The Autobiography of Malcolm X* (New York, 1966), 278–81.

7. Andrew Kopkind, "The Birth of Black Power," *Ramparts* (October 1966), 4–8. Interviews with Stokely Carmichael and Alvin F. Pouissant.

8. Bob Clark, "Nightmare Journey," *Ebony* (October 1967), 120–30. Interview with James Forman.

9. *Liberation*, April 1968, 3–8.

10. Michael J. Arlen, *An American Verdict* (Garden City, N.Y.: Doubleday, 1973), 93.

11. Robin Morgan, *Going Too Far* (New York, 1977), 123–24.

12. Susan Brownmiller, "Sisterhood Is Powerful," *New York Times Magazine,* 15 March 1970, 26–27; Shulamith Firestone, *The Dialectic of Sex* (New York, 1970), 72. Interview with Susan Brownmiller.

Chapter 13

1. P. J. Boyer, "Big Guns," *The New Yorker* (May 17, 1999), 54–67.

2. *U.S. News & World Report* (August 15, 1994), 34.

3. *Newsweek* (May 10, 1999), 35.

4. *Ms. Magazine* (January/February 1989), 84.

5. Interview with Carolyn McCarthy.

6. *Good Housekeeping* (September 1996), 64.

7. Interview with McCarthy.

8. *People* (December 30, 1996), 110.

9. This and the following from McCarthy interview. *New York Times,* October 7, 2002, A12.

10. *New York Times* letter, 13 July 2001, A-20.

11. Interview with McCarthy.

Chapter 14

1. *Compassion v. Washington*, 79 F. 3d 790 (9th circ, 1996); *Washington v. Glucksberg*, 521 U.S. 702 (1997); *Vacco v. Quill*, 521 U.S. 793 (1997). Interview with Ramona Ripston.

2. Quoted in A. L. Woolbarst, *Medical Record* (May 17, 1939).

3. Sinnard and Bloom Personal Declarations were made in support of the state of Washington in the Glucksberg case, August 2, 1994 and July 29, 1994, respectively. Interview with Barbara Coombs Lee.

4. *Journal of the American Medical Association* 270 (1993): 870–73.

5. Seneca quoted in Charles Moore, *A Full Inquiry into the Subject of Suicide*, vol. 1 (London, 1790), 270.

6. Joseph Fletcher, *Morals and Medicine* (Boston: Beacon Press, 1960), 191.

7. AARP publications: "Older Americans 2000," Indicator 1, Appendix A; Indicator 25; *Health Affairs: The Policy Journal of the Health Sphere 20*, no. 2 (March 2001).

8. This and the following paragraph are from Daniel Callahan, *Setting Limits* (New York: Simon & Schuster, 1993), 130, 143, 215, 228, 240.

9. *Manchester Morning Union*, 5 January 1950, 7.

10. *In re Quinlan*, 70 N.J. 10 (1976).

11. *Chicago Tribune*, 21 September 1976, sec. II 4, 1

12. *Cruzan v. Director, Missouri Department of Health*, 491 U.S. 261 (1990).

13. Luis Kutner, "Due Process of Euthanasia: The Living Will, a Proposal," *Indiana Law Journal* 44 (1969).

14. John Taylor, "Haunted Bird," *New York Times Magazine* (July 15, 1991), 24.

15. Peter G. Filene, *In the Arms of Others* (Chicago: Ivan R. Dee, 1998), 188.

16. This and the following four paragraphs from an interview with Derek Humphry.

17. Timothy E. Quill, *New England Journal of Medicine* 324 (March 7, 1991): 691.

Chapter 15

1. For this and the following paragraph, see Quill, *New England Journal of Medicine*, 691.

2. For this and the following nine paragraphs, see the *New York Times*, 6 February 1992, A-21; 4 May 1994, A-16; 20 August 1996, A-13; 23 November 1998, A-12; and 24 March 1999, A-20. For CBS, interview with Philip Scheffler and *New York Times* letter from Don Hewitt, 25 November 1988, A-24.

3. *New York Times*, 8 August 1972, 15.

4. This and the following two paragraphs from California Assembly Committee on Health, Interim Hearing, October 8, 1974, and interviews with Barry Keene, Ramona Ripston, and Anthony Beilenson.

5. This and the following four paragraphs from James M. Wall editorial, *Christian Century* (August 21–28, 1991), 763 and October 30, 1991), 988 and *Commonweal* (special supplement) (August 9, 1991), 46. Interviews with Tony Green and Claire Simons.

6. *Compassion in Dying et al. v. Washington*, 85 F. 3d 1440 (1994). *planned Parenthood of Southeastern Pennsylvania v. Casey*, 947 F. 2d 682 (3rd cir), 21 October 1991.

7. For this and the following five paragraphs, see *Connections* 8, no. 2 (fall 2000) and *Connections* 9, no. 2 (fall 2001): 1. Interview with Barbara Coombs Lee.

8. For this and the following five paragraphs, see, among frequent articles in the *New York Times*, 25 November 1994; 1; David Garrow editorial, 6 November 1997; 19 November 1997, A-18; and 21 April 1998. Also see *The Oregonian*, 24 January 1998, p. 1. Interviews with Monica Knorrs, Barbara Coombs Lee, Charles Porter, and Estelle Rogers.

9. For this and the following paragraph, see Al Karr, "Oregon Suicide Law," *AARP Bulletin* (October 1998), 9 and letter to Reverend David Hubner from Lee, October 25, 2001.

10. For this and the following three paragraphs, see the *Washington Post*, 24 February 2000 and 9 November 2001 A-1; *The Oregonian*, 9 November 2001, 3; and the *New York Times*, 23 April 1998, A-1. For the *Chicago Tribune*, see *AARP Bulletin* (December 2001), 11. For Rothstein, see

Compassion v. State of Washington, 850 F. Supp. 1454 (Washington, D.C., 1994).

11. For Glucksberg and Vacco citations, see chapter 14, note 1.
12. For Colombia, see *Compassion Newsletter* 7, no. 2 (August 1999): 4 and *Sampson v. State*, 31 P. 3d 88 (Alaska, 2001).
13. For this and the following paragraph, see Filene, *In the Arms of Others*, 206–9 and the *New York Times,* 29 November 2000, A-3 and 12 April 2001, A-16.
14. For this and the following paragraph, interview with Dion Aroner.
15. Robert N. Butler, M.D., *Why Survive? Being Old in America* (New York: Harper & Row, 1975), 421–22.

SELECTED BIBLIOGRAPHY

For those interested in the history of ideas, there are two books that stand above all others: Joseph Fletcher, *Morals and Medicine* (Boston, 1960) and Glanville Williams, *The Sanctuary of Life and the Criminal Law* (New York, 1968). David J. Garrow, *Liberty and Sexuality* (New York, 1994), is also essential. In addition to the following list of key works, the bibliographies of my own books on birth control and abortion rights might be consulted.

Bacciocco, Jr., Edward J. *The New Left in America*. Stanford, Calif., 1974.

Blanchard, Dallas A. and Terry J. Prewitt. *Religious Violence and Abortion*. Gainesville, Fla., 1993.

Blanshard, Paul. *American Freedom and Catholic Power*. Boston, 1949.

Broun, Heywood and Margaret Leech. *Anthony Comstock*. New York, 1927.

Calderone, Mary S., ed. *Abortion in the United States*. New York, 1958.

Callahan, Daniel. *Abortion Law*. New York, 1970.

Carmen, Arlene and Howard Moody. *Abortion Counselling and Social Change*. Valley Forge, Pa., 1973.

Chesler, Ellen. *Margaret Sanger, Woman of Valor*. New York, 1992.

Davis, Flora. *Moving Mountains*. New York, 1991.

Davenport-Hines, Richard. *Sex, Death and Punishment*. London, 1990.

Dworkin, Ronald. *Life's Dominion*. New York, 1993.

Ehrenreich, Barbara. *The Hearts of Men*. Garden City, N.Y., 1983.

Ehrlich, Paul R. *The Population Bomb*. New York, 1968.

Ellis, Havelock. *Studies in a Psychology of Sex*, vol. 2. New York, 1936.

Faux, Marian. *Roe v. Wade*. New York, 1988.

Flexner, Eleanor. *Century of Struggle*. New York, 1973.

Fryer, Peter. *The Birth Controllers*. New York, 1966.

Gebhard, Paul H. et al. *Pregnancy, Birth, and Abortion*. New York, 1958.

Hodgson, Jane E., ed. *Abortion and Sterilization*. New York, 1981.

Hoff-Wilson, Joan, ed. *Rights of Passage*. Bloomington, Ind., 1986.

Howe, Mark DeWolf. *The Garden and the Wilderness*. Chicago, 1965.

Kaiser, Robert B. *The Politics of Sex and Religion*. Kansas City, 1985.

Kennedy, David M. *Birth Control in America*. New Haven, 1970.

Kinsey, Alfred C. et al. *Sexual Behavior in the Human Female*. Philadelphia, 1953.

Kopkind, Andrew and James Ridgeway. *Decade of Crisis*. New York, 1972.

Lasch, Christopher. *The Agony of the American Left*. New York, 1969.

Luker, Kristin. *Abortion and the Politics of Motherhood*. Berkeley, 1984.

Mansbridge, Jane J. *Why We Lost the ERA*. Chicago, 1986.

McWilliams, Carey. *Witch Hunt*. Boston, 1950.

Miles, Dudley. *Francis Place*. New York, 1988.

Nuland, Sherwin B. *How We Die*. New York, 1994.

Pfeffer, Leo. *God, Caesar, and the Constitution*. Boston, 1975.

Pincus, Gregory. *The Control of Fertility*. New York, 1965.

Powledge, Fred. *Black Power, White Resistance: Notes on the New Civil War*. New York, 1967.

Reed, James. *From Private Vice to Public Virtue*. New York, 1978.

Schulder, Diane and Florence Kennedy. *Abortion Rap*. New York, 1971.

Select Committee (1819) of Sir David Evans, 585. *Parliamentary Papers*, vol. 8, p. 43.

Storer, Horatio R. *Criminal Abortion in America*. Philadelphia, 1866.

Tribe, Laurence H. *Abortion*. New York, 1990.

Vogt, William. *The Road to Survival*. New York, 1948.

Webb, Marilyn. *The Good Death*. New York, 1997.

Zinn, Howard. *SNCC: The New Abolitionists*. Boston, 1964.

Index